Faces of Foster Care

Messages of
Hope, Hurt
and Truth

LISA AGUIRRE

WESTBOW
PRESS®
A DIVISION OF THOMAS NELSON
& ZONDERVAN

WestBow Press books may be ordered through booksellers or by contacting:

WestBow Press
A Division of Thomas Nelson & Zondervan
1663 Liberty Drive
Bloomington, IN 47403
www.westbowpress.com
1 (866) 928-1240

ISBN: 978-1-9736-3426-3 (sc)
ISBN: 978-1-9736-3427-0 (hc)
ISBN: 978-1-9736-3425-6 (e)

Library of Congress Control Number: 2018908371

Print information available on the last page.

WestBow Press rev. date: 07/23/2018

This book is dedicated to Jervon. I am so proud of you.

Contents

Preface..ix

Felicia 1
Joe 7
Kellie 15
Dayar 21
Leah.. 30
Madison.. 38
Chris.. 44
Kendra.. 59
Christine... 68
Sarah 74
Pam.. 83
Dominique.. 92
Tessa 94
Charell 99
Brittany 109
Sarah 114
Julia... 118
Schylar 125
John 132
Nathaniel 138

Epilogue.. 145

Preface

For the last few years I have been volunteering with a wonderful organization in Washington D.C. called the Family & Youth Initiative (DCFYI) that works to match mentors and potential adoptive parents in foster care to older kids (teens and young adults). A caring, committed adult in the life of a kid in foster care can make all the difference between a life of struggle, or one of success. After getting to know some of the kids in the program I learned how great these kids are, and how tough life can be for them. But I also saw resilience in them beyond anything I had witnessed before, and that's why I am committed to making people more aware of older kids in foster care. It's the reason I wrote this book. Within these pages you'll find stories of people across the country who grew up in the foster care system and went on to become successful, contributing adults, as well as people who interfaced in other ways with the foster care system.

For this book project I met with twenty people from around the country, including former foster kids, social workers, adoptive parents, and a child welfare administrator all of whom were involved in some way with the foster care system. I did not ask specific questions; rather, I just made them aware that the project I was working on was intended to raise awareness about older kids in foster care. They were free to talk about whatever they wished. The format was informal and meant to reflect the messages as communicated by the participants. Also, I included the person's first name and the current state they live in, though several were involved with foster care in other states.

So many people encouraged and supported me throughout this project. Family were my biggest cheerleaders, especially my husband Wilde Aguirre and my kids Naomi Studtmann, Omar Aguirre, Daphne Aguirre, Kami Khan, and Fiama Aguirre; my sister and her husband Josette and Todd McMichael; my mother Vivian Votipka; my aunt and uncle Mary Ann and Edmund Mauzy and my aunts Pauline Gross and Pam Votipka. I thank Sandy Leap, Michelle Ferry, Tawni Schwemer, Penny Hawker Smith, John Studtmann, Debbie Studtmann, Nicole Khan, Saif Khan, Becky Fuchs, Harold Aguirre, Selenè Aguirre, Ryan Upperman, Lidia Mitacc, Jessica Lmr, Maura Olimpia Castillo de Aguirre, Manuel Cesar Aguirre Castillo, Martin Alarcon Lòpez, Pilar Alarcon Lòpez, Carmen Guadalupe A. Aguirre de Alarcòn, Kendria Navarro Clark, Morgan Montgomery, Monica Ray Gruntkowski and Sonia Irma Parodi Antayhua for their endless encouragement and support. Marisa Lue Chee Lip, Katarina Ayala, Naomi Studtmann and Daphne Aguirre worked tirelessly and diligently to transcribe the interviews. Susan Punnett of DCFYI continually encouraged me and provided many referrals as I was seeking people to interview. Thanks to Pastor Barry White who has talked for so many years about the importance of finding your God job, which I feel I did with this project. Lauren and Diego Boccaleone wrote an excellent article on this project in their blog, fulltimetired.com, and they encouraged me throughout this project. My gratitude also goes to adoption.com for doing a first-rate feature on this project on their website. Cupcake Heaven and Café provided great coffee and the perfect atmosphere for working on the book. Finally, biggest thanks go to Christine, Joe, Felicia, John, Schylar, Kellie, Dominique, Brittany, Madison, Pam, Kendra, Nathaniel, Charell, Chris, Pam, Leah, Julia, Tessa, Sarah of MT and Sarah of D.C. for their willingness to meet with me and speak out publicly through this book to raise awareness.

I worked on this project in my spare time, entirely outside of my regular job with the U.S. Department of Health and Human Services (HHS). This work is my personal work and is not affiliated with HHS, and the messages in this book are those of the participants. All profits from this book will go to DCFYI (DCFYI. org). In the twenty stories below you'll find heartbreaking pain and moments of triumph, learn about the nearly insurmountable odds foster kids face in terms of quality of care and trying to establish a life beyond the system, and you will discover how the face of child welfare in this country can change for the better with a shift in focus and allocation of funds.

Felicia

Washington, D.C.

School was everything to me. I always loved going because I loved learning. In second grade I was a math whiz and memorized my times tables before the rest of the class which meant I started getting invited to math bowls and competitions. But the next year, in third grade, something happened which precipitated a transition. I was seven, and after loving school and never wanting to miss a day, things changed. People in our building and in the community started to notice something was wrong; neighbors started asking questions. They weren't being nosey, exactly, because if it weren't for them, my life would have taken a much different route. So I'm thankful they were actually aware of what was happening with me; that's a great thing about neighbors.

When I came home from school one day in the third grade there were a lot of police cars in front of the building. The school was literally right across the street from where I lived so I didn't have far to walk. *What is going on?* I had no idea it involved me; after all, the building had about thirty units. I saw the police and a police car, and they told me to get in the backseat. I asked, "What is happening?" You know, they don't tell you anything; they just take you. You're young; they don't want to talk to you.

From there, I was at the police station, and someone—I don't remember who—came and took me back home. That was the first time, and once you are in a situation like that, they don't stop monitoring you. It happened again—the neighbors called the police after suspecting things weren't right. There was a lot of arguing and, you know, fights in the house. That was another reason to keep an eye on the household. Finally, I started knocking on a neighbor's door for food. It had been a couple of days, and I hadn't eaten. That was also a sign to neighbors that something was happening again in the household. So the cops came again, and they took me to the precinct and started filing papers. I was removed from my home. It was a long process, and I don't remember all of it. But that was when they put me in the foster care system. The system can be challenging. It can be difficult to place four siblings together. I was in three different schools during third grade—three different schools at the age of seven. The third home seemed okay at first; it seemed we had a family.

The problem though, is that sometimes people start to remind you of how much worse your situation is than it used to be. They start saying bad things, and you want to defend yourself. I was not always in a positive environment as you'll see a little bit later, so adults didn't get a positive reaction from me. I guess I was rebellious because of what was happening around me, so I was removed from that home. At that time I was entering the sixth grade and once again had to move into a new foster home. I was still in the system, just under kinship care with family members.

At this time I was old enough to say yes or no to adoption, so I said no. I moved from house to house because I was acting up. You know, things were just crazy. They took me from my family, and although they kept saying we would stay close to each other, that did not happen. I started thinking, *I just want to go to school; you know, reverse the curse of what is happening in my life.*

I entered foster care at the age of seven and exited at the age of twenty-one. In the New York foster care system they put you through college, but once you are finished with college, that's it. You are on your own. College changed my life. I got a mentor, someone who pushed me through school. I had a good social worker, a woman I call my aunt to this day. She was at my graduations from college and graduate school. Over the years, I had multiple social workers due to various changes, but she was the main one who acted like family to me. She didn't act like she was just my social worker; she wanted to make sure I succeeded. She actually took the extra steps, as many others do, to make sure I excelled, and I feel like I have. I know for sure that college is the way to go. It is important to just get there, and everything will work itself out. I am a true testament of that.

During my college experience as a foster youth I moved from New York to go to college in South Carolina. Once there, I became very active in organizations and found myself in leadership positions. I joined a sorority. I started a foundation to help people strengthen their math skills. I was favored by a lot of professors, and they really respected me. I never openly announced I was a foster youth, but I did receive some education funding, which made me very happy. The times when family had to bring me back to school after summer breaks were hard because I didn't have anyone to help me transition. However, my college graduation was the ultimate best. I was so happy, because my immediate family, extended family, foster parents, and friends were all in attendance.

Once I finished college I got an apartment in New York City, in Manhattan. Even though I was close to certain family members in the Bronx, I did not visit frequently. I was reminded of the past when I went to their houses, because even though they were physically there, they were not really there, because a person is in another state of mind when he or she has an addiction. The addictions for these family members were drugs and alcohol. Thinking about it reminds me of how the back room in that place was closed off to everybody, but I knew what happened in that back room. Even when I did go there to try and visit, they would be in the back room with many other people and never come out. Obviously I am not naïve; I knew exactly what was going on. But I always acted like I didn't know. Just because I didn't see it, doesn't mean I didn't know.

If I have kids, I will not let them be around anyone who is a bad influence; they are not going to be around that. It's not that I think I'm better than anyone else. Instead, I want to protect them. No one should have a memory of such a negative environment. I told certain people they would never see my children if they didn't change their ways, and I would not feel bad about it at all. They are not going to grow up seeing this and having thoughts and bad dreams about what could happen. I told my family members they had to get themselves together.

As for my life after I exited foster care, after graduating from college I moved back to New York. The transition was a little difficult. It was hard to get a job in New York; I was living by myself, so I started tutoring students in math because I needed money and couldn't wait for a job, so that helped pay the bills. I did that for a while.

Eventually I moved to D.C. for graduate school, worked full-time and did tutoring on the side while taking graduate classes. It became too much and I got expelled for having an F in one of my classes. When you fail in graduate school they just kick you out. I thought I would be able to handle all that I was doing, but it became overwhelming. I did appeal the school's decision to expel me, but they require you to wait a year before starting school again. Ultimately, being kicked out turned out to be a good thing because it was during that year I started my own math tutoring organization. Part of the proceeds go toward scholarships for college students to help pay for college books and care packages. We do these on an application basis, first-come, first-served. They get a nice package with portfolios, planners, résumé paper, business cards, bed risers, and pens. I'm a big fan of organizers and planners. I love organizing; that is what keeps me sane. Our organization is nationally known now. A few people from California applied recently as well as some from Florida. They received care packages and scholarships. Next year we are planning to give $30,000 in scholarships, and all of the proceeds came from tutoring.

During that year off from school I sent the dean an e-mail almost every day, updating her on what I was doing so she would know I wasn't just sitting around, that I was working. I told her I started my own organization and that I was ready to benefit from the master's program. I was ready to give more to it and had more knowledge and experience, so I could handle it. Finally, the appeal went through, and she let me come back and I kept my scholarship, so that was great. After I got back in, I got all A's, and the dean even asked me to start talking to new students about my experience so they wouldn't go through the same thing.

I graduated with my MBA, and now I'm an adjunct professor at a university here in D.C. I am also still running the tutoring organization, and it continues to grow. I feel very fortunate to be where I am, doing what I am doing. Foster care was a real challenge for me. For years, I couldn't talk about it as openly as I do now, but I learned that the more you talk about it, the more you heal from the experience. People say I act like it doesn't affect me, but if only they could know what it was like over the years; it really did affect me. Now I'm more in tune with myself, and I don't blame anyone. After my past and the path I came from, I see that I am truly blessed to have been a part of the system, because my life could have been very different. I can't change where I've been, but I thank God for always protecting me and listening to my prayers. I am happy that now my sisters are growing closer and that my mother and father are focusing on the betterment of themselves and finding themselves. The move to D.C. was a great idea. I am happy I decided to change my environment, meet new people and get more mentors.

Joe

New York

I am a father of five; all were adopted through foster care. I grew up myself in foster care and aged out without being adopted. So, the experience I wanted to give my kids was a greater sense of permanency, I made sure they knew that living in my house was permanent in a legal sense. That makes a difference for me, and I am certain it makes a difference for them.

That piece of paper means a change; it says you belong somewhere. I don't know why there is a huge difference about it for me because it doesn't really change the relationship, but it is just something to hold onto. When growing up in foster care I had been neglected, so later I searched and found out everything I could about my past. I am talking about finding official papers like health, court and school records. I have always been the kind of person who needs to have something tangible, so that is probably why I wanted to adopt my kids and not just foster, that makes the relationship undisputable. The truth is, you can say lots of things, but that doesn't necessarily make it all true, so the legal permanency was important to me.

I grew up in a family with six children, four of us were foster children and two were the biological children of my foster parents. There were other foster kids in and out of the house over the years. I never had one hundred percent certainty that I wouldn't be the next one that had to leave. Thinking back, though, I wasn't going anywhere, but as a kid you don't know. There was no explanation for the kids leaving. They would come, they would play there for a few months or so and then all of a sudden someone would come and pick them up and we wouldn't see them again. My fears that I may be the next to leave were just reinforced. So many social workers came to visit us, the various foster kids, that it caused confusion. I remember wondering as a child why no one else I knew had this type of situation at home.

My siblings and I also went to school with five different last names. We all had our biologically given names, and our foster parents had their last name, so there were always questions, always reminders. I was always one to talk about it, which was an issue with my family. My brothers would say, "Mom, he is telling everybody!" It wasn't really a secret anyway. My foster mother was Caucasian, and we were all children of color. I'm biracial, there was another brother who was biracial and the other two were African Americans. So, it was like, *hello*? It was an obvious question; it was an elephant in the room. When you see an elephant, you talk about it.

Eight years ago, when I was fifty, I decided to become an adoptive dad. I worked in foster care for many years as part of my professional career, and never during that time did I decide to foster or adopt. I even remember doing home studies for families who wanted to foster or adopt, and I thought to myself, how do you do this? The issue for me always involved financial concerns. Is it enough money to take care of the child? Will I ever have enough money to provide for a child in a way that I would like to provide for a child? That sort of ran around in my head for most of my adult life. It took me a really long time, and part of me wishes I had done it sooner, but the reality is I am where I am supposed to be.

My first son was seventeen when he moved into my house and eighteen when he was adopted. Initially, everything was fantastic, really, really good. So good that I thought, well, how about another kid? So, I talked with the first one about it, and he was not really into it at first which I understood. He wanted me to himself.

The second child was fifteen when he moved in and was adopted. The three of us were good, and sometimes those two would gang up on me, which I understand happens with typical parenting. Then, I just couldn't stop. There was a fourteen-year-old who needed a home, and I also adopted him. Then, there was a twenty-year-old with special needs who was about to age out of foster care, and no one really did anything to prepare him for aging out, so he became the fourth one. Now, eight years later there is a thirteen-year-old with special needs, the youngest that I have had, and there is another one I am thinking about.

In a period of eight years, we have become a family of six. You know, I guess I have absolutely lost my mind and my friends think I'm crazy, but I do this because I can. Everything I have done professionally has been about taking care of kids, and it has just been my passion. This all has come in the twelve years since I retired. When I was planning to retire, I was thinking of moving to Puerto Rico and relaxing. I worked in the public-school system as a counselor, so I had off in the summers and I just started thinking of my retirement as a forever summer. But, when I really started thinking about it, I started to feel incredibly selfish. I couldn't see myself sitting on a beach every day reading a book, or going for a walk, or doing something else that is just not useful. I could do something much more useful and have an impact on a child in foster care.

I was not thinking about saving the world. We always act like society can only deal with foster care if we are superheroes, if we have magical powers, and there is something incredible that happens that gets us to the other end. There are all sorts of fictional characters that we adore who have gone through foster care or adoption and there is always a wonderful ending and they are okay. But most of us don't have stories like that. Although the world has been very kind to me, I'm still not a superhero, you know, I still hurt. We look at the stars for our way to deal with foster care and adoption instead of looking across the street or across the table, so we don't see it. You don't need to be a superhero to be a foster parent, and you don't have to be a superhero to adopt a child.

If there is a kid that needs something, it is very difficult for me to look the other way. I would say it is almost impossible for me to look the other way. There were many years when I sort of rejected my upbringing in the foster care system. I am not anything like anyone else I grew up with. I have certain strengths. I am grateful I survived enough to be able to see my strengths and understand them.

I could tell you all of my personal, horrible stories about growing up in foster care, but I am beyond that, and when I talk to my kids about it, I need them to know that was my past, not my present. It is still a part of who I am because I still hear the little boy's voice advise me every day when I interact with people, but I don't allow it to overwhelm me. If it gets to be too much, I usually pick a spot on the wall, the beginning of the wall and I say to myself, do you see that little sliver, that first part of the wall? That is my childhood, and I point to the entire rest of the wall and say, that is the rest of my life. In hindsight, it is now like watching a movie. I'm not living in it anymore. You know, I think it is very important for kids to understand that someone suffered before them; someone cried before them, but most importantly, that someone survived. Those examples of survival or resilience are what give people hope.

I could throw a cape around my shoulders and run around in the street, but I don't think that is going to give anybody any hope. I think that in my situation, what works well in my family is that no one comes from another world. We all went through foster care. We don't allow each other to put all our pain up on a wall and frame it, because no one else … well, I'm going to use this word, but I think you'll understand what I really mean … no one else really cares because we each have our own pain. The pain is not allowed to be an anchor that they can drag across the floor. There is no one in my house who didn't grow up in foster care, who doesn't have their own story, and who hasn't lost a parent. I think that approach works really well for us.

We do go through our stuff though. You know, my kids had no concept of Father's Day, and I had this fantasy about a perfect Father's Day, so it was a big disappointment. There were times I just had to get in my car and take a drive, grumbling under my breath because things hurt my feelings. But they get it now, because I called my friend to vent and then he called them and said, "Look, you guys have to do something for Father's Day." Also, Christmas was not a miracle on Thirty-Fourth Street either. I mean, kids grow up in foster care in a way where everything is given to them no matter what. So, earning something is not really a concept. When I try to talk about it, they ask, "What do you mean? You are supposed to give me this or that." I have one of my kids, for instance, the year before he moved in he had eight different pairs of glasses. Yes, eight. I am glad to say that he has had the same pair since moving in with me six months ago. He is on his third phone, but at some point, he will need to learn. I don't always know how to un-teach some of those things they learned without there being actual consequences. It is easier just to pacify them, but that is not the lesson I want them to learn. So, those lessons are also my lessons because I have to live through the consequences of me imposing consequences, and I have to just laugh to myself sometimes.

One of my struggles over the years was that at times I desperately wanted to know who I am and where I came from. That was because I was so different from everyone else I grew up with and I had never met my biological family. I always wanted to know who my mother was and was on a quest for many years searching for who I am, really ever since I can remember. When I was in college, maybe eighteen or nineteen years old, I contacted one of the social workers I knew and asked if she could find some information about me. I had never been adopted so my records weren't sealed, and through her I was able to collect a little information about my biological family. It wasn't a lot, but I did find one name and a birthdate. It took many years of looking to finally find where the person lived. The reason I couldn't find it sooner is because she had gotten married, and under New York State law marriage records are not public information.

I was in my mid-forties when I finally found out where certain family members lived. It was actually in the same school district I retired from. I was born in the 1950's on Long Island, and it was just a different time. My mother is Caucasian and my father is African American. That was not a good thing back then, and the family hasn't really evolved. But, it is what it is. When I wanted to contact my family, I reached out to one person in particular because I had found her contact information. I sent a letter and pictures to her along with my resume. I sent everything about me, and I was so proud of who I was. I recall very clearly the day I received her response. I was working at the time and I just grabbed the mail quickly as I ran out to catch the express bus. I was on the bus flipping through the mail and I saw the response so I opened the letter. I couldn't believe what she wrote, and I was just devastated, so much so that I was weeping on the express bus. She had essentially written me an abortion letter; saying I should have been aborted. She totally took everything that I was and who I thought I was and in an instant, destroyed me. I mean, there have only been a couple of times in my life where I have been that out of control. I was so naïve about how they would feel about me; and maybe naïve because I thought I was this wonderful person and they were going to love me. But she didn't. I call it the abortion letter. It was devastating.

I could go there in an instant now and start crying. Everything that we are as people is about connecting to something, to where we come from, who we are, and she threw it on the ground and stomped on it. I learned a good lesson about my vulnerabilities that day; that I was more vulnerable than I thought. It was probably one of the most hurtful things that ever happened to me, and the hurt was inflicted by a family member. To this day I sort of try to defend her actions in my mind, thinking, well, she is old, so she grew up in a different time, and she had it rough. With my letter, all of a sudden the big secret came out and she just lashed out. Her response was horrific. I mean, there is no other word for it. After reading her letter I remember walking around in a state of shock, it was almost like losing someone in an accident. I thought I had found my family, but I was numb, and I was lost again.

Ultimately that, like other things I experienced, made me a stronger person. Would I have loved to learn these things a little differently? Of course, but I don't think I would be the person I am and doing the things I am doing if I had not gone through that experience. You know, I spent an incredible amount of time trying to find out who I am and where I belong. It was an obsession in childhood because I wanted to belong somewhere, and it wasn't a great fit in the foster home I grew up in. After I received that response, I still spent years trying to learn about my history. I mean, I really can't tell you the hours and hours I spent trying to find out who I am. Finally, I was able to go back many generations on both sides and learn about them.

I found out there is French royalty way back on my mother's side. This was very empowering for me to learn. On my father's side, I found a narrative about my second great-grandfather who was a slave. He lived in Virginia and was married with three kids. All were owned by the same person, but then the master sold my grandfather's wife and kids and kept my grandfather, so the family was separated. After the emancipation many years later, my grandfather went looking for them. At that point his children were older and married. My grandfather walked or did whatever he had to do to search for his family and ended up eventually finding them in South Carolina. So this man, who was a newly freed slave, did something miraculous and went looking for and later found his family. It had been many years, and both he and his wife had remarried, but he found her, and he found his kids all in South Carolina. My goodness, the power behind that story.

I grew up with none of that passion for family, and when I read that story I felt so empowered by it because that is what I would like to think I would do. That is who I am, too. To be able to say that I am like my grandfather after nothing but emptiness for all of those years is absolutely incredible to me. You know, I have so much pride in who he was and, you know, the other side of the family with royalty. Having that information is like being home; there is some security in it. I have a place in history, in time. I belong, and a lot of times growing up in foster care I felt that I didn't belong. Just to know that I have a history, I belong somewhere and I am not a mistake, it gives me purpose and a sense of calm. In terms of my kids, I want them, too, to feel like they belong somewhere. I want them to know I am here for them and they can say, "That is my father."

Kellie

Kansas

Let's see, I have a master's in social work, and I work with youth who are aging out of the foster care system, who are transitioning out of care. I am an independent living program manager. We work toward figuring out what it is they want to do post care, whether that's going to college, or setting them up in an apartment and finding them employment. Basically, helping set up their path as they age out of foster care.

I'm also a rapid responder for human trafficking, which entails a four-week rotation, seven days a week, twenty-four hours a day on call. I got called out this morning around 12:45, and I was out until about 5:00 a.m. We partner with the Exploited Missing Children Unit here in our county. Law enforcement does the biggest part of the interview, and then I go in and assess safety, provide physical and mental health recommendations and make a shelter recommendation. This could mean emergency care, a foster home, or otherwise figuring out where the youth wants to be placed or if the youth has an interest in going back home. It all depends on the severity of the situation.

For this morning's call, she was actually a youth who was in the foster care system who had been reported as a runaway. So, I had the opportunity to chat with her. She wasn't very talkative because it was early, and she was tired. That was an interesting case, primarily because law enforcement didn't have enough to justify her as a trafficking victim, but she is at a very, very high risk for trafficking due to her circle of friends and environment.

I find that really sad, because I think those are the youth we struggle to help find the right services and support for. They don't meet certain, and at times unrealistic, criteria to be, I wouldn't say locked up, but placed in a good home until child welfare professionals can figure out what it is the youth needs to be doing so they can get away from that toxic environment. Basically, we had to bring her back into the office due to a lack of foster homes and she ended up staying the night at the office. I hate that! I don't know. I'm trying to be cautious with what I'm saying because I am a social worker, but I do think there are some flaws in the foster care system that could definitely be improved.

I do have a fairly positive view of foster care just because it really saved my life. As a former foster youth myself, it gave me the opportunity to go to school and get a master's degree. I mean, it paid for the bachelor's, not the master's. I'm still in debt for that, but it gave me the opportunity to further my education and to really become someone. My whole life, I have always been focused on education, and I feel like it has come full circle helping others because people once helped me.

The system and the professionals that were involved when I was in care had more of a positive role versus a negative one. Of course, there were some negative aspects to when I was in care, and I worked from thirteen all the way up until now. I paid for everything I needed and wanted. I did not have the best foster home, but it was a good one and I did only have one foster home. I know in that way I was very lucky compared to most youth my age at that time. So, I felt very fortunate to have only one home, especially when I know that if that home had been different it could have impacted where I am today.

I was born and raised in Wichita. I lived here for twelve years when I entered into foster care and was moved to a small town in Kansas. It was literally three to four hours away from Wichita, really far. It was actually a culture shock for me because we lived in a city and then I went to this very small town of less than one hundred people.

I would say that coming into care was the most traumatic part of my whole life, regardless of the abuse in my biological family's home. I think that being moved away from the only things I knew was way worse than what I experienced at home. I say that because I think the system and the professionals struggle to help youth understand what is going on at that time, and instead, they are—and reasonably so—focused on finding placements and figuring out where the kids should go. But they neglect the fact that these kids are being ripped away from the only things they know, their families, regardless of what was going on.

We forget to just keep them in the loop of, you know, where their sisters went, where their brothers went, where everyone went at the time they were being separated from everyone. We don't tell them who these foster parents are they will be living with. I now know they're not just random people. They've gone through training, and while that training could be improved, these are not just random people you are being thrown to.

We don't do the best job of keeping youth informed at each step, especially if they are not going back home, or they are not going to be adopted. We have exit plans as they exit care. We do adoption reports and stuff when youth get adopted, but we just don't do a very good job in terms of when kids come into care. Shouldn't there be an intro plan for the child? It's my understanding there is an intake process.

You know, we gain information from the child and family members, bombarding them with question after question so we can provide services and support to the family, but we don't do the best job of focusing on the youth, focusing on keeping them informed about what is happening and what's going to happen next, that type of thing. I have seen workers neglect to tell a youth they would be moving to a new placement. I feel like that's just not right. They are going to be ripped away from the thing they know and they will have a new home, need to adjust to a new environment, and everything else that is involved.

I also think one of the biggest struggles with the foster care system is that we are not able to maintain placements. I think, at times, we make it easy for foster parents to say, okay, I'm giving up on you and you are going to go somewhere else. What we really should be doing is providing better support to the foster parents during those times. I mean, it's not their fault either. They may not have had adequate training or knowledge to be prepared for that youth. I get that.

I am coming from both sides now, from the side of a former foster youth and from this other side of social work. So, my perspective has changed dramatically over the years, especially as I continue to work in child welfare. At one point I probably had a kind of negative viewpoint of foster care, but still very appreciative because of the college experience I was able to get. But now I feel like my whole experience was almost more positive than anything because I can also see what the professionals face.

They are doing the best they can with the knowledge they have given the information they can obtain with the limited resources they have. I applaud so many social workers, therapists and lawyers; I want to cry because they are all doing the best they can. Sometimes it is just not enough. This is so, so sad because these kids deserve so much more than we can give them. You know, sometimes for some children and families it just may not be enough. I don't know, it's just sad. I wish I had a good answer to all child welfare issues.

I am motivated by a thought I've shared with former foster youth: there is always someone better than you. One of my foster parents said that to me once when I was playing basketball. They meant it in regards to the game, but I've applied the concept to life ever since. At the time the foster parent said that to me he was probably being mean, but it was motivating to know there is always someone better.

So I strive to be my best self. Some people might see that as tiring, for if there is always someone better, why try harder? But for me, I just continue working harder and trying to be better and I encourage youth with that same message. You can't just give up because life gave you the wrong lemon. You have the choice to make a better decision, to make a better path. I think a lot of youth struggle with the life handed to them, and they struggle to see that they can make lemonade. That's so cliché to say, but you know, you can make something of your life or you can continue to fall backward and let life drag you down. I've always been someone who uses the hard times as fuel to keep moving forward.

I have always been fascinated with the words 'fighter' and 'resilient' so my other message is to just keep fighting, because no one else is going to do it for you. You have to want to do it and you have to want to be better and to do better and have a better life. There were people during different periods of my life that helped me and made such an impact that they helped propel me to where I am today. I had a school counselor who helped me a lot in terms of finding scholarships and figuring out what resources were available to me as I was aging out of the system.

The social workers I had in care were not the best, but the independent living worker was. This is the worker assigned once the case is opened post care, for kids who have aged out of the system. Mine really helped a lot while I was in college. She bent over backwards and manipulated numbers just to help me with my plan. There were days where I didn't have a lot of food, so she was able to help me get groceries and she helped with rent.

Over the last several years, I have been really reflecting on my past and on my story, and where I am today. There are still times, nearly every day, when I question why I am where I am. As former foster youth, our voices need to be heard. Even if what is shared is negative information about the system, it is still data, so it should not just be dismissed just because it's negative. If you just look at the positives, you are never going to improve. I think there is a message in the negatives. But it is also important to acknowledge the positives because there is this negative notion of the system. Like I said, I had some workers and professionals who impacted my life greatly.

Child welfare is just so hard to improve and change because you can make an improvement that might be a positive impact on twenty kids, but it might negatively impact ten. It is hard to pinpoint what needs to be changed that will positively impact the majority.

I recently got married to a wonderful man who I've been with going on eight years now. He is amazing. He is motivating and inspiring and he just takes me for me, you know? He challenges me to look at things differently because I am a pessimist at times. I may not have a clear picture of something, or I might not be seeing everything, and I feel like he plays the part that helps me realize something I wasn't seeing or even looking for. I love him to death, and I can't imagine my life without him. I hope all foster youth find that person who really helps them because they are at such a high risk for re-victimization and toxic relationships. I just hope everyone finds someone like I found. I'm just really lucky; really, really, lucky.

Dayar

Washington, D.C.

I'm twenty-three currently, and grew up the majority of my life in foster care. I was formally introduced at the age of six and then removed from my family. But in terms of having an open case, of being in social services, that was a year before I was formally placed into the system. When I was placed into care I didn't know everything that had transpired before.

I learned these things when I was much older, and now I realize if I had known about them earlier, the knowledge would have helped shape me differently. There's an early memory of coming home from school and seeing one of my family members sort of upset and packing my stuff. I recall seeing two other people at the time; a police officer and I guess a guardian ad litem, which is basically the advocate for you, your foster care lawyer if you will. I remember that particular time of going into care because one thing stuck out to me that day, it created an absolute hatred, a dislike for all white people. Not because a white person had done me harm or physically abused me in any way prior to this incident, but the person I saw before me, removing me from my home and family, was a white person. So this feeling wasn't necessarily racist, if you will, but I definitely had animosity towards Caucasians or white, fair-skinned people and it showed up in the way I responded to them. I felt more comfortable with a person of color. This experience shaped my view, and I didn't know at the time what I know now. I just saw this person as white. It could have been a black person removing me from my family, but in this instance it was a white person and I saw her as the cause of me being removed from my family.

Life was hard even prior to being removed from my family. My sister went into foster care a year before I even stepped foot in the system or knew what the system was. I didn't fully process not seeing her at that young age. I just knew she was not there; I wasn't with her anymore. I still got to see her a little, but she wasn't with us, and then I was removed. I recall having visitation rights with my family very early on. One thing stuck out to me on every visit. Certain family members used to tell me this was short-term. We are going to get you soon, they'd say, and at the time this was something I really truly wanted to hear; that the stranger's house I was living at was only temporary.

But telling a child at that young age that you're coming to get him and then not showing up, I think, was the hardest to take. Who was I to believe? My family or these people I'm temporarily staying with? How I looked at it was, I don't need to take this, I don't have to do what you say to do. My family is coming to get me soon. Those thoughts soon reflected how I acted. I was very standoffish with the people I stayed with in foster care and I exhibited really aggressive behavior. I used to really act out and

I just thought the more I acted out the sooner I might be able to move back in with my family. But at the time, I knew or thought my family was working towards getting me back.

I kept thinking I had a family; I'm not like one of those kids in foster care. I am a regular kid, and I have family I can go back to at any time. They are just doing stuff until I come back. That's how visits used to be. I distinctly remember the visits. They used to be great visits. They used to always tell me, "We're coming to get you. It will only be a little while longer." Or they would say, "It's the social worker that doesn't want us to have you. It's someone else." Once again, it happened to be another white person who moved me. So to me, all my traumatic experiences and the reason why I couldn't be with my family wasn't because it could have been a bad placement, it was because this person didn't want me to be with my family. They didn't want me to stay; they didn't want me to be happy.

It was years later, as I got older, my lawyer and guardian ad litem began to tell me more. They had this big file of all my records. That was the first time I was actually told why I was in foster care, and I had been in care at least five years at that time. I was twelve or thirteen. Prior to that, I had bounced around in over twenty-eight foster homes, group homes and multiple other homes.

I remember being in a pre-adoptive home that fell through. I was like a teeter-totter, but that wasn't uncommon for me at the time. I was self-destructive if I thought things were going well. I did not want to be adopted, but this was the goal of the system and they sort of force you. You can't make your own conscious decision; they don't think you have the ability. They tell you what you are going to do; it was always adoption. Having a separate family was something I never in a million years would have thought I'd want. I had my family. They were not perfect by any means, but they were mine, it was something I had. It was my family. People I knew, people I grew up with, my blood. Why would I ever want to have a second family when I already had one? This was a hard concept for me. If they would have actually asked me, I would have told them.

At one point after I had been in a few pre-adoptive placements that fell apart my guardian ad litem said they found a placement. I think they thought this placement was really good for me and the person looked really good on paper. This was one of the first times I was actually happy for a little while. I wanted to be a part of a family. My guardian ad litem saw me teetering and then slip into how I used to behave. Then things didn't look good for the placement. I recall my lawyer sat me down and explained how I came into care. Now that I look back on it, it was one of the worst and best days of my entire life. It was hard to realize and come to grips with the fact that I was not going back to my family, that this was not something that was going to happen. To tell a child, I was a child then, just going into my teenage years, that everything I had been dreaming about and hoping for was actually a lie, was life-changing. When I learned that going back to my family was not something that was going to happen, it was extremely heartbreaking.

I have never shared this with anyone, but when she told me that I made a vow to myself that I was going to find a home and I was going to make the situation the best I could make it. That, I knew I could do for myself. I wasn't going to let anyone else make decisions for me. I wasn't going to let anyone else decide for me. It was finally a decision I got to make. I didn't need my social worker's approval. I didn't need to talk to my guardian ad litem about it. I didn't need to consult with my foster family. It was a decision I made for myself.

This was a changing point in my life. After the foster family I was with ended up being disrupted and I was removed, things changed to where I felt like I was in control. There wasn't anyone else telling me, "This is what you want" or "This is your goal." I came to understand a lot about myself during this time. I began to understand things that I hadn't understood before. Finally, a light bulb clicked and suddenly I was in the light, and I knew. I had officially within myself determined that I was going to be adopted. I was going to find my forever family. While I might not have my biological family, it didn't mean that I couldn't have a family.

Looking back on it, those experiences in foster care and going through the process made me who I am today. They shaped the type of work I want to do. I have done a lot of work with a self-advocacy nonprofit on how to be your own person. The moment when I was finally told everything about my past, I didn't know it would really affect me. It was just information, but it really truly changed me and shaped me into who I am today. I can see that now, looking back. It changed how I saw things, how I operated, how I viewed my family a little. For a while I was angry with my family and I couldn't figure out why, I was just angry. It was years later that I was able to pinpoint why I was angry. I was angry because they could have just told me, but no one wanted to share that I was never coming home. I could have been with six families less. I could have been happy and stable. I could have been somewhere. My family, they didn't think about me. They didn't care enough about me to allow me to have that happiness, to allow me to even have that glimpse of happiness for myself, or the opportunity for it. Every time they told me it was okay, I believed them. For a long time I believed them, even after my guardian ad litem told me everything. A part of me believed my family and what was happening couldn't be true.

That was also the time I decided that maybe it wasn't entirely the agency's fault, it was not just this white person taking me away, it was something much deeper. I didn't know it at the time, but it was those moments in foster care and growing up that built who I am and laid the foundation of where I wanted to go. I understood that I couldn't do it myself. I began to build a network, to make friends. I didn't shut people out anymore. I needed them, not in the sense that this next person I met was going to be my adoptive family with a happily ever after ending. Rather, I saw it as a situation I just needed to make work for now. I built a network of people to propel me to where I wanted to go. But, while I wanted to create and maintain relationships, there was also a level of isolation and aloneness because I wanted to keep everything to myself and not allow someone to have too much power, too much information, or too much ability to control me. I wanted to be in control. I wanted to decide how much they knew and how much they would help me.

I set up walls, and while I knew a lot of people and had formed a lot of relationships, the relationships were contingent upon whether I thought they could help me get to my next level. I never outright said those things, what my intentions were, but I would have an extra mentor on stand-by when the one I had couldn't help me in a certain area. I began to create relationships to have more people that could to help me get somewhere rather than just having relationships with people to help me, if that makes sense. It was the only way I saw to get the things done that I needed to do. I came to understand that while I wasn't physically, financially, or otherwise able to do for myself, I had created this network that could help me. That worked for a while. It worked for a really long time.

I don't know what changed, what made me switch, but at some point I realized that I had all these people in my life, but I was still missing one thing. I wanted a family. I wanted to be actively involved in the adoption process. I wanted to know the people. I wanted to screen them before I was sold off like an auction item. Shouldn't I have the right to know who wants to adopt me? Shouldn't I have the right to know who they are? Shouldn't I have the right to meet them before a decision was made that this would be a great fit for me?

I began to get more involved with the adoption process. Most people want to adopt a little child five or six years old. I was seventeen or eighteen. I was turning into an adult and there are not many options for older adoptions because a parent wants someone they can parent. How do you parent an eighteen-year-old? They are set in their ways and mostly already shaped into the person they are going to be. Many people want to adopt when they can still shape a kid. It was a difficult moment when I realized there weren't many families out there beating down doors to adopt older kids. That became an issue. Why don't people consider older adoptions?

That was traumatic. No, it wasn't traumatic. I don't look at all of it as traumatic, even though there were some traumatic moments in foster care. I look at those more as growth points; points I was able to learn from and use to propel me to success. They created a persona of something greater, that my current situation wasn't the end all, be all. I could do much better. I could strive for much better than my family. I could finish high school. I could go to college. I could be successful.

I guess I can talk a little about being adopted at a much older age than anyone would normally think of or consider. I was adopted a year ago, when I was twenty-two. When I was adopted, it was a good experience to be a part of a family. At the same time, it was a really rough experience to be part of a family. I say that because by this time in life I had already reconnected with my biological family. Also, over time, I had created my surrogate family. I had my Godparents. I had a family, not in a traditional sense, but I had people I considered my brother, my sister, my aunt and uncle, my parents, my moms. You notice how I have an 's' after mom, my mom wasn't just one person. Mom was multiple people. When you're adopted, it shrinks down to the family you're coming into. It was no longer my moms and my dads. It was my mom, my dad. It became singular. That was really hard to deal with. I wanted to still be connected to the people I considered my family, but I also wanted to be in this new family.

Even now, I'm still trying to figure out the balance of how much is too much and how much is too little and understanding the dynamics between these relationships. For example, I have these other people who raised me and I call them mom, but I realize I have a biological mom, and I know her. To take it a step further, I have my biological mom who is no longer legally responsible for me, but I know her. It is really awkward. Who do I call when I'm really down? Do I call the woman who adopted me? Do I call my biological mom? Or do I call the other ladies that helped raise me and shape me?

I think that's the trickiest part of being adopted at a much older age. I had already developed so much into who I am and formed relationships that have become part of me. I've been figuring it out, taking it one step at a time. There have been a few hiccups, but it's been a great experience, certainly a learning experience.

I guess I can talk about my adoptive mom and how that relationship came to be. I met my adoptive mom at an event held by a local non-profit organization that helps find mentors and potential adoptive parents for older kids in foster care. We talked about it later, and I didn't remember meeting her there. Then, I had to go to the DC courthouse for a school project and she works there, and I saw her there. I had to go to the courthouse often and because I knew she was there, I would ask her if she could help me out, show me around. We'd hang out and grab lunch, and chit-chat while I was waiting. The relationship started out as me going to her job for a school project, and that blossomed into a mentor relationship. That soon blossomed into her fostering me, then that blossomed into her adopting me. It started out as a regular person that I didn't remember meeting and it turned into something completely different.

It happened to be a circumstance that I never thought of. She's white and Jewish. I'm African American and Christian. What were the chances that I would come across this person and make a connection in a way that would develop into a relationship like this? I am really grateful for it, and I'm glad that things happened for me in a way which made it so I wasn't angry with white people anymore. I could have missed having my mom if I still carried that anger and resentment. I'm thankful for that. I'm not thankful for the way in which I learned that, but I am thankful that things worked out great on my behalf. It's something I'm really happy and proud of.

I think one thing foster care has given me and taught me is a level of resilience and a high level of joy. It taught me to always see the brighter side of things and to find a small crumb of happiness in every situation or every person. If it weren't for foster care, I probably wouldn't have those attributes. It's the circumstances

I went through in foster care that helped me become successful and to be a senior in college now. I have been able to experience what most foster youth in D.C. don't have the opportunity to experience. While I didn't have the best upbringing, I made the best of what I had. I made lemonade out of my lemons. Sometimes a little more lemon is added because everything isn't so sweet, and there are some bitter times. Even with adoption and being stable, life does still give you lemons. There were times in foster care that I had bad experiences. Times where I felt really down, but there were also times after I was adopted and when things were stable that everything wasn't just peaches and cream. I learned to not necessarily just go with the flow, but to look at the positives, not to focus on the negatives. If I focus on the negatives, I will never be able to move forward. If I allowed the things that happened in my past to determine where I am going in the future, I would never be able to wake up and get out of bed.

I feel like my story isn't just my story. My story can help someone else who may be in the same situation, someone who went through the same experiences that I had in foster care and even outside of foster care. Who am I not to share my understanding, my insight, and my struggles, so that they won't go through those same struggles? I feel like it's not just my story. It is my job to help someone else out with my story, to share it as much as possible and to be proud of my story.

Leah

Washington, D.C.

I was looking for somewhere to volunteer, something to do to give back in some way. Several years before I had heard a young man testifying at a Senate hearing about having been in foster care growing up. His testimony really affected me. He had been in several foster care placements. He talked about not being included in family meals; the family ate at the dinner table and the several foster kids in the home were given a plate and had to sit on the stairs to eat their meals. He talked about one placement where he could have breakfast or lunch, one or the other, but not both. He talked about a placement where he was given a bag of potato chips for his birthday.

His talk really affected me. I was so impressed by how together he was in terms of his presentation, because it must have been very emotionally challenging to talk about such things. He was really well spoken, really emotionally together, very poised. Poised is probably the strongest word. I went up to him afterward, gave him my card, and told him if he ever wanted an internship I could help. He actually took an internship at the State Department instead of with me, not a totally ridiculous choice. But we kept in touch. One of his skills is that he maintains connections and builds a sort of safety net for himself, and I think it was this skill that helped him through foster care.

We got to be friends, so when I happened to mention I was looking for somewhere to volunteer, he said there was a small, local nonprofit organization that helped older kids in foster care. The volunteers work to find mentors and possibly adoptive parents, and to just make sure that when a foster kid ages out of the system they have a responsible adult connection. That sounded interesting to me, though I had no idea what it was going to be like. To be honest, I thought that the kids would be cynical, jaded and possibly hostile. I had a lot of preconceptions and almost none of them were right.

I thought I would start by going to some of the group events, and maybe I would eventually be a mentor. I went to my first event and got to know two kids. I met several kids, but there were two who actually talked to me more than the others, a young man named Dayar and a young woman about the same age. One of the things I really noticed at that event was how affectionate they were with one of the volunteers there. I think she was a mentor to the girl and was just good friends with Dayar. They were walking arm and arm with her at the zoo. I was surprised because I think many teenagers are afraid to show that type of emotion or affection.

I got to know the two of them a little bit there, and I learned that Dayar was in culinary school and had an interest in cooking.

That is sort of a hobby of mine, so we talked a lot about what we liked to cook, and our favorite food shows on TV. I thought it was a good conversation. I also appreciated the adult volunteers and I felt like they were sort of kindred spirits. I liked the sense of community the organization had. So I kept coming to events and I met different kids, and I would also see Dayar and the girl again. Then toward the end of the year, Dayar's biological sister started attending events. In some ways they have very different personalities, but I really enjoyed getting to know her, as well. We also did several things together outside the official events.

Soon after that, about a year after I had attended my first event and met him, Dayar asked the head of the organization if I could be his mentor. I talked about it some with her because he didn't seem to need a mentor. He was good at collecting people and keeping in contact and he had a lot of mentors. He did not seem to need a mentor as much as his sister did, since she was new to the organization. But on the other hand, he had taken the initiative to ask, so we could not quite figure out what made the most sense. Ultimately what we decided, because at the time I had a lot of time on my hands, is that I would mentor both of them.

I was very excited to be a mentor, but interestingly, almost immediately I thought to myself, wow, I want to adopt this young man. Dayar's sister did not want to be adopted, she was adamant about that, but I knew he did, even though at the time he was in college and about to turn twenty. I started seriously thinking about it. I did not tell him what I was thinking, because if I were to decide against it, I did not want him to feel any rejection. It took me a few months to make my decision.

While I was thinking about it, I remember going to dinner with a friend and I asked if I could bring my new mentee along. After dinner, she said, "You should adopt him." I was shocked (and pleased!) by her reaction and told her I had actually been thinking about it. Prior to that comment, I had been thinking that my friends would think it weird that I would adopt a teen, never having parented. It was very reassuring to have a friend suggest something that I was already thinking about, and she didn't even know I had been thinking about it. I hadn't told anyone.

Several weeks after that, I remember exactly where I was when I became sure of my decision. I was driving down Massachusetts Avenue, crossed over Wisconsin Avenue and had just passed the Cathedral when certainty came to me. I am going to do this. Then a big smile came over my face and the decision just felt right. I was so sure of it.

So, I told the director of the organization my decision and that I wanted to start taking foster parent classes. A foster child must live with you for six months and you must be their foster parent during that time before you can adopt them. I started taking those classes, and then I felt I needed to tell my parents. They already knew I had two mentees, but they didn't know I was thinking about adoption. When I first told them they had a million questions. Have you thought about this? Have you thought about that? You know, they asked all the very practical questions about college financial aid and health insurance, and all sorts of things. You know, parent questions.

It took a couple days to think through all of their questions. I do remember that at the end of that first phone call, despite all the questions they asked, my father said, "Whatever you do, we are going to support you. We'll be there. We'll be there for you." My mother said, "Of course we will." Then she said, "Wait a second, if he is going to be my grandson, I want to meet him." So we agreed that I would come out to see them the next month and I would bring him with me.

When we went to visit my parents it turned out my aunt and uncle were also visiting. So Dayar got to meet a whole bunch of family members all at once. The minute they met him, they were sold. They were completely sold. It just became like a mutual admiration society, him and them. After that, one day he actually texted me and asked if he could move in at the end of the semester. That fall, he started spending weekends at my house. So it all happened fairly quickly. I started thinking about all of it in the early spring, made the decision to adopt in late spring, finished foster parent training in July, and then that fall he said he wanted to move in by December, which he did. At that point, he still wasn't aware that I wanted to adopt him. I wanted to wait until he brought it up, until he felt comfortable with it. The whole move-in process was smooth, and it was a very brave thing for him to do because he had been living with his prior foster mother for a while and they had a good relationship. He was treated well there, and it was clear they were genuinely concerned about him and loved him. I think he worried about their feelings about his decision. Also, once he moved, they would get a new foster child and there was no going back, so that is why I say I think he was brave.

The first several months were definitely an adjustment period. I felt like I was constantly being asked why I did things a certain way. It really felt like criticism to me, but I think he was just puzzled because things were done differently, and it was a challenging time, you know, as you sort of adjust to each other. I think most of us don't think about the fact that families have informal rules like, this goes here and that goes there, and if we're going to be late we call or, you know, we always wash the dishes after dinner or we don't have to wash the dishes after dinner. We don't always realize we have these rules.

About two weeks after he came to live with me I was walking from my car to my house and was held up at gunpoint. They demanded my purse and my keys. I had never been a victim of crime before. I think I had my bike stolen in college, but I had never really been a victim of a crime like that, and there I was looking down the barrel of a gun. So early on we were dealing with a really traumatic situation on top of the fact that it was all new and challenging anyway. I think it certainly taught us a lot about each other and we each got to see how the other person handles being stressed, angry and scared. I do remember a day or two after that incident I was wondering if I had the ability to do it right; to parent him well. I asked myself if I could do it. Did I have it in me? It wasn't that I didn't want to, but I think the stress of what was going on at the time made me question whether I had it in me. But that was the only time I even vaguely questioned my decision. That was, if not quite a turning point, at least a significant moment. We knew there were going to be some challenging times, but we are in this through thick and thin. Once we got through that, we found our equilibrium.

We went on a few college visits before he moved in, and maybe once after he moved in because he was about to finish up his associate's degree and planned to transfer to a four-year school. These campus visits required some traveling, and we found out we traveled very well together. That is important thing to know if you are going to be family members.

So in December he moved in and that next August he went away to college. I remembered my mother talking to a friend of hers years ago whose child was going away to college. My mother said something to her about how you can't cry until you turn around and walk away from them. I was stunned. I hadn't realized the day I went away to college was a sad day for her. I was surprised, because at the time I was so excited to be going to college. It was the most exciting thing ever. I hadn't even thought about the fact that was a really difficult day for my parents.

I took Dayar to school and got him settled into his apartment. I was there for a couple days just to make sure he was settled, and I started crying even before I said goodbye to him. He went to his first class and then afterward we met for lunch. My eyes welled up right there as we sat in the cafeteria. Then we went to his apartment and I handed him his first care package. I had thought of what I was going to say, some meaningful parent message, but by the time I was composed enough to say it he was walking away with the care package. We said our goodbyes and I got into the car and pulled just a little bit away from his apartment and then parked. I texted my parents: How did you do this? I'm crying my eyes out! My mother responded, "Yeah, tell me about it. Both of us cried a lot too when you went to college." A little while later they told me Dayar called them after I left. So he had said goodbye to me and then he called them, which was interesting, touching.

Dayar had been with me for about a year when he finished

his first semester and started his second semester. During the second semester he went on a school trip for spring break and I went to visit my parents as well as my brother and his wife and kids. We were all together. Dayar texted me and said he had a question he wanted me to think carefully about, and that he was asking me right then because I was with my whole family. His next text said, "Would you want to adopt me?" I just teared up and showed my mother his text. My parents had actually been waiting for it to happen, but I had told them that it would happen only when and if he was ready. My parents were really thrilled. So it actually went pretty quickly because by this point he was already twenty-one. He had aged out of foster care, so there weren't as many checks because he was not legally a child. He asked me that question in March or April and we finalized the adoption at the end of May.

We went to the courthouse for his adoption ceremony. The court had technology so family and friends who couldn't make the ceremony in person could still watch it. We had about a dozen family members and friends with us, including Dayar's sister, so we had a large group of people filing into the small courtroom. There was a TV screen on the wall. Dayar and I looked at it and saw four small boxes on the screen, picture-in-picture boxes. My parents were in one, my brother and sister-in-law and their dog in another, and my two aunts and uncles in the other two. All of these people are spread out over thousands of miles, yet they were all able to be there at the ceremony. It was really something for both of us. We were really touched by that, and it was so nice of the court staff to get it all set up like that.

The ceremony was relatively quick. I had similar but not identical necklaces made for the two of us with a favorite quote of mine from an E.E. Cummings poem: *i carry your heart with me, (i carry it in my heart).* Then the entire group, along with a few others who weren't able to make the ceremony, went out for a big dinner that my parents covered. They wanted the group to be together for a really nice meal. So we all sat at this long table. It was really a special day.

We've had all sorts of adventures since then. A little over a year after he was adopted we happened to be in Toronto for the weekend and all of a sudden he asked if I wanted to get matching tattoos. He, being in his early twenties, has several. I didn't have any and had always been scared of the process and thought it might be painful, but I was so touched by the idea that I said yes. He started talking about what the tattoo would look like and that he wanted to have the adoption date in the matching tattoos. So we did that, and mine is on my right leg and his is on his left. They don't look identical, they both say Love and have the adoption date, but his tattoo is much more elaborate and fancy. I got simple writing, meaning thin letters because I was too chicken to do too much filling in, I was afraid it would hurt. It really didn't hurt that much; and I love my tattoo. The fact that he wanted to get the tattoos was a very meaningful thing.

Certainly, there have been moments when I wanted to scream—he can be a typical twenty-something—but I have never regretted my choice. Never. Mostly I just feel really blessed, and I feel like there is so much more love in my life because of him. He does things that are just really touching, and I will probably start crying if I talk about how good he has been to my parents. I think in many ways my family is just like others, you know? Sometimes we are great and we have a lot of fun, and sometimes we annoy each other, but we are absolutely one hundred percent there for each other. Dayar has become an essential part of our family and has shown that he is there for us one hundred percent, and we are there for him. I feel so fortunate that my path led me to him and he wanted me to be his mom.

Madison

Nevada

Well, there is a lot I want to talk about. One specific conversation that is not being had is about older youth who have to make the difficult decision to choose adoption or post-foster care services. So, I will give you my story. I entered care when I was ten years old. I was in care for seven and a half years.

During that time, I went through seven different homes and as many different schools. At seventeen I was adopted, it was six months before my eighteenth birthday. It was kind of a difficult decision because I had spent so much time in care. I would have been eligible for post care services to help financially support me until I was twenty-one, but I thought it would be a better idea to leave foster care with a forever family, a forever home. So I made the decision to get adopted when I was seventeen and a half. Unfortunately, my relationship with my adoptive family fell apart a couple weeks before my eighteenth birthday. So when I was eighteen I basically found myself in a pretty difficult predicament; without either a family support system or the safety net of government services. Since I had been adopted, I was no longer eligible for any services.

A couple of days before my eighteenth birthday I moved into this decrepit motel in Vegas. It was a very terrible place and was eventually shut down because it was so bad. I had a little graduation money, so that helped sustain me for a couple of weeks. I got a job at the library and that helped pay some expenses. My independent living worker, who was not required to give me any services, gave me bus passes.

At that point, my biological mother had passed and I was not close with any family members, so it was a very isolating experience. From the age of eighteen until now, I still don't have a relationship with my adoptive family. You know, it's really difficult because a lot of people don't see the challenges I had to go through to get to this place in my life.

If I were to raise awareness about anything, it is how important it is to make sure older kids do not need to choose between either being adopted, or receiving government services, because it puts them in a very difficult predicament. We want to advocate for a forever family, but we also need to recognize that a forever family might not actually be forever. We also don't want our kids to be crippled by becoming too systematically dependent on the child welfare system to sustain them. So, I don't know, it has become very difficult because it is hard for me to advocate on either side. I want kids to find their families and have a support system, but knowing what my experience was, I know that is also the experience for a lot of kids.

I think these kids are a very invisible population. No one talks about the situation, because if you talk about it then you have to acknowledge that sometimes adoptions fail and there is no system in place to catch those kids, especially if they are older when they are adopted. If a kid gets adopted at twelve and the adoption is dissolved at fourteen, that kid still has time to maybe find a new forever home, or at least they will have some time before they age out of the system. But for older kids that get adopted, if the adoption fails, they are faced with a world of uncertainty. They don't know what to expect. If I have any message to share it is that I wish kids didn't have to choose between adoption and post care services. Also, there needs to be a better support system for the kids that might not have one. My message to them is to just keep going, keep fighting.

Something else that's important is that we need to make sure there is enough support for birth parents. There are assumptions in foster care that birth parents are evil, they're demons. It's us versus them. A lot of people come from this judgmental place about birth parents and oftentimes it does more harm than good. When someone is criticized so much, they can lose the spirit to do better or be better.

My mom had a third-grade education and she was from Vietnam. She actually emigrated from Vietnam. My father also emigrated from Vietnam. My mother was half black and half Vietnamese, and my father half French and half Vietnamese, so I am racially ambiguous. My mother had very, very dark skin and very tight curly hair. She was ostracized in her home country and lived in an abusive situation. Then she came to the United States. Growing up, we lived in trailer homes, other people's houses and shelters to include domestic violence shelters. That's how I grew up.

My mother couldn't speak English and was not very educated, so we were always running away from abusive situations. Running away from it, but then running back to it, because domestic violence is very complex. It's not as easy as just deciding to leave, especially when you have children to feed and you don't have any skills, and you don't speak the language of the land you live in. It was very difficult for my mother to be a single parent, but she always made sure her children were fed, that her children were cared for.

There were a lot of cultural differences. In Vietnam, there were no parenting classes; that's a very American concept. As a frustrated mother trying to discipline unruly children, she physically disciplined. So, when the initial report came into child services the first response was to remove all of her kids. But what they didn't really realize at that point was that she was financially stable, had a really good job, and we were living in a house for the very first time. We had never lived in a house before.

My mom often relied on me to help interpret or write documents for her. So, when they removed her children, this woman who didn't have a preexisting drug addiction, had never really been homeless and had never solicited before, was so struck down by depression that she went down all of these pathways because she didn't have familial support. We didn't have any family in the United States and she was separated from her children. For a woman who came from a different country, she couldn't comprehend how a government agency could just come in and remove her kids and not tell her where her kids were. After that, my mother was really stricken with depression. She didn't have much support, and the only people who would support her were friends who were drug addicts.

Something I generally say about my experience is that foster care did me pretty well. I had the opportunity to go to college for free. I got to meet a lot of people. I get to travel for a living, especially in the field of child welfare. I would never have been able to do that if I didn't enter the foster care system. But I do always say that the foster care system broke my mother.

She didn't have the support she needed. She didn't have the resources. She didn't understand culturally why her kids were removed. My mother struggled for the next fourteen years. She died about two years ago. Based on what I was told she always loved her children, she just didn't know how to get her kids back. It wasn't as simple as going to parenting classes, going to visitation and being a better mom. She was a non-English speaking woman who couldn't communicate to her employers this concept of foster care and that she had to do x, y and z in order to get her kids back. So, it just led to one thing after another. Once her children were removed and she started participating in the case compliance, she got fired because she was missing work. The next consequence was homelessness, and the next consequence was drug addiction. Then the next consequence was trying to find a man to take care of her because everything else had fallen apart.

Anyway, one thing I always say is that we need to make sure we provide support to our birth parents. Each birth parent is one decision, one mistake, or one bad day from getting their kids removed. Some people have the support and resilience they need to get their kids back and some people don't have anything. When they don't have anything, they are going to go down a much darker path than many of us would choose.

I know if my kids were removed I would do everything in my power to get them back, but I have a different level of resiliency and a support network that would make me successful. My mother didn't have any of that. She wasn't a drug addict, but after her kids were taken away she became one. All of this makes it very clear to me that support is such an important thing in helping make people successful. I am almost certain that if my mother had relatives that had taken her children in, and she knew that her kids were safe, and she understood what was happening, that things would have turned out very differently for her and for all of us.

It's kind of hard for me to explain what I do for a living because I don't have just one job. For my full-time job, I work for a non-profit that provides support to kinship caregivers, and I am the child welfare and program development director. I manage their training programs including kinship caregiving, CPR, preventing child sex abuse, and car seat training. My other hat within that position is their development, so that means grant writing, donor management, donor development and managing interns. So that's what I do on a regular basis. Outside of that, I'm a contractor and I do child and family services reviews. I am also a general young adult consultant, so we do technical assistance for states on child welfare items. I do LGBTQ training for child welfare professionals and am a foster and adoptive parent trainer. I also work with the rape crisis center in delivering a curriculum to reduce and prevent child sex abuse.

If I had to tell older youth in foster care something, I would say that it gets better. I mean, it only gets better if you see that there is a light at the end of the tunnel. I'm twenty-six and I own my own home. I have a pretty good career and am financially stable. I have assets. You know, I'm doing pretty well for myself. But I didn't do it on my own, either. Even though I didn't have a traditional family, meaning a biological family or even an adoptive family, I created a support network of mentors who could help with various things. It's about recognizing that you can get a little bit out of everybody to help build what you don't have. I would just encourage people to be resourceful, vigilant, and resilient. Just know that you're able to overcome any obstacles as long as you are able to fight for another day. It's not easy, but I just take it one day at a time and know that there is a light at the end of the tunnel.

Chris

Pennsylvania

I have told my story a thousand times. I don't talk about what happened before foster care, just during and after foster care. I have parents that are still alive, and I don't want them to have to deal with it. I have gained a bit of notoriety, so they have already had to answer some questions so I generally keep them out of it. And, I smell like a chimney, so beware.

I didn't mind foster care. I liked it. I got lucky. My stepdad was a cop, and therefore all the cops I grew up with felt the need to take care of me. So when I was placed in care they let me live in a couple of different homes until I was sure of the one I wanted to live in. I picked the one with old people, the oldest couple that they had because I assumed that old people were senile and not attentive to what was going on. It was the complete opposite. They were right on it and they were strict. The dad woke up every morning at four, and the mom would wake up with him. She would iron his jeans. I didn't think that people actually did that, but she did.

I already had a work ethic before I got there, working in greenhouses and selling things. For example, one of the guys who was good at basketball in my town broke the backboard in the gym and I scooped up all the pieces and sold them on the way to the bus. He was somewhat of a local celebrity. I made about one hundred dollars. I've always been that guy; they called it hustling back then, but now it's entrepreneurial. I was a hustler. I had the kids in my lunchroom who were adorable little kids undersized for their grade go around to all the senior girls and tell them they forgot to bring their lunch money. Then, when the girls would give them their lunch money, the kids would come to the table and we would split it all up. We did this every day for a whole year. Nobody ever caught on because they were so adorable, or maybe because they were poor, who knows? We would then go play pinball with the money because it was the kind of pinball that X amount of credit was for X amount of dollars. So, you could double, triple or quadruple your money in the afternoon doing that.

I got to the old couple's house, saw their work ethic and so I worked too. I did all kinds of odd jobs and eventually worked with cleaning big machinery. And that was from right after school until three the next morning. I would then go home and say hi to the couple because they were up getting ready to go to work, and I would grab three hours sleep and then I would go to school. I did that for a long time. That guy paid me under the table and sometimes he would pay me with WWF tickets. I would give them to my foster dad because he liked that.

I met a lady who was many years older when I was in my senior year of high school. I had a job at a gas station and she lived across from the gas station, so she would come over and flirt with me all the time. Eventually, we started dating. She was old, and I was nineteen. It was weird in that regard. She was twice my age. Anyway, my foster dad at this point was in his late sixties, he was beyond the age of retirement. He was only working because he was still taking care of us, me and my foster brother who had just graduated. My foster brother was going to college and was going to move out really soon.

I thought to myself, *I am the last kid here and I'm a bigger guy. I have always been tall, so my clothes take a little bit longer to wash. I take a little bit longer in the shower. I eat a little bit more than the average person.* I started to think that my foster dad spent a lot of money on me, and this girl really likes me. So, I decided to move in with the girl. That day was very movie-esque. It was raining, and my foster dad and I were driving down our country road. My foster dad said, "You don't have to do this." I said, "No, it's okay. I don't mind. You need to retire." I had my trash bag of stuff and the whole nine yards.

So I went to live with this girl and I continued going to school because it was two weeks until graduation. I thought I would be graduating soon, so I figured it would all be fine. Then I got called into the vice principal's office, and he told me I couldn't play basketball anymore. He said I had lost my eligibility because I had moved out of my foster parents' house. He called me to his office and asked, "Where do you live now?" I said, "Oh, I live with this girl and it's great." He asked, "Do you pay rent?" I said, "No, all I do is show up. Everything is paid, and I'm fed and it's great." And he says, "So you have no bills in your name?" I said, "No, I have nothing in my name." So, he told me that I couldn't prove that I live there, and if I couldn't prove that I lived there, then I couldn't prove I lived in the school district. So, I got expelled.

I was really sad because this was the longest I had been in one school since I got into foster care. I was at that school for maybe two and a half years. I was getting ready to go to prom and getting ready for graduation. Then I was told that I couldn't do any of that. I got to see the graduation, I just wasn't in it. I had a party for prom night, but I did not get to go to prom.

I cleaned out all of my stuff from school. I had most of my things from my life in my buddy's car. I hadn't quite taken it all to the girl's house yet. I didn't want to bum rush her house. I figured I could just move with changes of clothes and whatnot, and then leave the rest of the stuff in my buddy's car. So, I moved all of my stuff from school into his car too.

When I went home to that girl, I said, "You are never going to believe what happened to me today." She replied, "Well, you will never believe what happened to me." She had been offered a job in Michigan and she was taking it. I told her I wasn't going to Michigan; we had only been dating for a few weeks. I hadn't even really moved in yet. I wasn't going to move away from my support system. That would have been silly.

She told me I could stay there since the rent had been paid for a couple of months. There was no anger or animosity between us, until I started selling her furniture. She left it. I figured if she left it, she didn't want it and so I started selling it. But at one point later, she wanted it and it didn't go well. When a man came to get the furniture for her, I wouldn't let him have it. The police got involved.

I had a prom party because I had my own place. I also had a graduation party, but I didn't have much furniture left because I sold it all. I had wicker outdoor furniture inside the living room and a TV. That was all that was in the whole place. I don't even remember where I slept to be honest with you. Then one day the landlord came by and noticed I was not the lady. He told me I needed to go, and I said, "Well, that makes sense." And so, I left.

I did the couch thing for a while. Then my best friend's mom told me she had heard what was going on with me. She said I could live in her back room, and I would need to get my GED. I didn't really want to do either of those things, but they were very nice people and I didn't want to upset anybody, so I said okay. So, I got my GED, and then she enrolled me in college. College was great, but I had to pay the fees. I went to school long enough to play one season of basketball and then I was done. I didn't want to be there anymore.

When I left college I lied to get a job. I found a small newspaper that needed a graphic designer. I had no experience at all, but I told them I could do everything, that it was going to be easy for me, no troubles. He said, "Okay, this guy is going to leave so watch him for few weeks." I watched everything that man did. My roommate at the time was like a little brother. He is a big computer guy, and he had a program I could use. I would go home and mimic everything the guy at the newspaper did. I would make my own newspapers every single night until he quit. And when he was leaving he said to me, "You don't know anything." I responded, "I didn't when I started, but I do now."

I ended up working there for a while. I changed it from a small newspaper to an actual magazine for the community, and they gave it out for free. Another printing company saw what they were doing, saw that they were getting big, and bought it for big money. They did not bring me along with it, even though everything about it was me. That was the first I learned how cold the journalism world is.

I then started working with another newspaper and my job was to edit what the editor did before the story came out. My job was to have the very last look at this thing, and I guess I edited him too many times. A normal person would get better at their job over time, but he did not. So, he just lashed out at me, and I got fired for editing him too often. The whole job description was edit the editor. So he knew that's what I was there for. Anyway, this is what happens to us foster kids. I don't know if we have shifty eyes or something?

Then, my roommate moved out and I became homeless. I started working for a guy who had a dog kennel, so I could live above the dog kennel. He had all their vocal cords cut, so all night long I could hear tiny whispering uff uff noises. One morning that man came up to my loft area at seven in the morning to say, okay, let's go to work. I responded that we didn't talk about hours or anything, that I am not your call guy. Just tell me what hours you need me to work and I will work hard during those hours, but then I am done. You don't need to come up here at this time and tell me to do any of this. Needless to say, I didn't live there after that day. So then I called the SPCA and he did not live there beyond that day either. He lost his kennel, he lost his house. That was vengeful, but he was a terrible person. He just happened to be around a homeless kid at a time when a homeless kid needed somewhere to live, but he was a terrible person. He sought free labor and thought he was going to get away with it. I was raised by a cop, and then raised by two strong-willed old people. I don't play around. Even if I am homeless, I'm not going to be a punk. This is something foster kids need to know, if someone hires you, they do not own you.

So, for a while, I kind of lived where I could. I used to live off a dollar a day. I would have a bag of chips and a soda, and that would be enough to get me through each day. Then occasionally somebody would have a dinner they didn't eat and I would eat that. Some people would take me out to dinner because they knew I was in bad shape. Being funny was the only way I got through all that because nobody wants to hear you cry about your homelessness. You have to give a homeless joke and you're in good shape.

I then worked delivery jobs and stuff like that for a while, just a supplemental income. I didn't have a career and I didn't want one. I just kind of wanted to relax and just get by. Eventually, I thought I should get serious about life and then luckily, I met a girl who's now my wife. It was weird, after foster care a lot of things just kind of fell into place. I couldn't get a job in journalism after that editor thing so I took temp jobs. For one of them I was a greeter for car sales. You know, when you get those gimmicks in the mail that say this key could open something, or scratch off this thing and you could win a prize? People would come in and I would keep them from not killing anyone because it was a scam.

I would get them to talk about buying a car. I did that greeter job one time, and they came back six months later and asked if I wanted to do it again. They told me I was really good at it, so

I did it again. They thought I was so good they wanted me to come on the road with them. I said, "Since I'm really good at this you should pay me more." They said, "No, but why don't you try to sell cars? You wanted more money, this is your shot at more money." So I tried it out and I was really obnoxiously good. I ended up being the top salesman and made so much more money than I have ever made before. I bought all the DVDs I wanted to buy. I bought the TV I wanted and the car I wanted. I had money. I had three kids and I still had money. Nobody was starving, and I still had money.

I'm not used to having money at all. I don't like the feeling of having money, because I'm going to spend the money. My wife asked me what I was going to spend the money on. I responded, "Do you remember that magazine I started?" Eight years earlier I attempted to start a magazine focused on foster care, but you need to have a whole bunch of money to pay for the office first of all and then to pay for products. I had done a web ad and got forty subscribers the first day. But the web ads are super expensive, and although I got forty subscribers, there was not nearly enough money. I couldn't even print out a magazine for forty subscribers. It was the advent of email, but I sent a snail mail letter to each of those subscribers because I didn't want a response. I told each subscriber that if they promised not to sue me for taking their money, if I ever did start a magazine I promised to send it for free, forever. You will never have to pay for it. Nobody sued me. Eight years later I started the Foster Focus magazine and those forty people are still subscribers. I got a couple of letters from people who said they were one of the original forty subscribers, and they knew I could do it. They said they weren't upset that I couldn't do it then, just disappointed. I responded that I appreciated what they said, but I didn't really think that I was going to be able to pull this thing off.

To start the magazine the second time I took a chunk out of the money I had from selling cars. I sold a ton of cash-for-clunkers cars, which are good payment-wise, and then I sold a ton of trucks. When I sold a ton of trucks, I mean I was sending a fleet of trucks to different companies. Where one guy would sell one truck, I got credit for twenty. I did this consistently and they really liked me. I gave myself a stupid nickname in the car business. I used to call myself Straps and that name got me hundreds of sales.

So, with that money I started the first year of the magazine. And then after that year, I told the guys at the dealership that I spent eleven hours selling and then five or six hours every night working on the magazine and something had to give. I'll either quit, or you have to let me work on the magazine when I'm not dealing with customers. Because I was the top salesman they said okay, and so I did that for another year or so, I can't remember how long. That's how I paid for the magazine.

I started to get some advertisers and then the subscribers really picked up. You are supposed to get advertisers first, but I got subscribers first. I did everything backward, but it worked out. It's in year six now and I have won a number of awards. Run DMC gave me an award. I got to go to a Saints Camp and interview Jimmy Graham. Rosie O'Donnell directly messages me and stuff. It's a cool life, but I would have been perfectly fine to have a regular job because I wouldn't be doing this if I hadn't been in foster care, which is a weird thing to say.

As I got some notoriety with the magazine, people started inviting me to come out and speak at events on foster care. I noticed at these events there was more complaining than advocating. So, you can title my section of this book, The Trauma Olympics. I will talk about that. It's a phrase I claim. When you get a group of foster kids, former foster kids, foster parents, or social workers together, any of them, something happens. They call it The Trauma Olympics. They start competing to see who's had the worst life. It is the strangest thing, and if you had the worst life you win the gold medal.

But, this is something that holds us back as a group. You can't complain more than you advocate. When you do, The Trauma Olympics is exactly what happens, you start crying and whining. That's one of the reasons I tell people when I'm there to talk to them, I'm not there to inspire them, and I am not there to make them cry. The key to beating The Trauma Olympics is not participating; you have to stay out of the fray. It's nobody's fault. Everybody wants to know what everybody's story is, especially alumni of foster care and the kids currently in care. They have been telling their sad stories since the very beginning. They have been sharing their stories in the hopes that somebody is going to relate and then better the system. I have been at this for six years and very seldom does this not happen. There are a handful of speakers that could make you go home and make you look up some more stuff about foster care, but there are a very, very select few that can get action from their speeches.

Unfortunately, as the years go on the payments are getting smaller for speakers, if one is even offered at all. So, what you have is a whole bunch of people baring their souls for nothing other than the hope that they are going to inspire somebody that's there, but those there are mainly there because they were already inspired at some point. They are not going to wake up tomorrow morning and say, you know what, I've been doing it all wrong, let's start it all again.

I am starting to see former foster kids get exploited, and then you also have the ones that get too bold. I'm at the point that if I didn't have a magazine I wouldn't be getting invited to talk anywhere. I'm thirty-seven years old for crying out loud. Nobody wants to hear what it used to be like in foster care so many years ago. They want to hear what it was like two or three months ago, or they want to hear about the last ten years.

It gets scary because these kids aged out of care, and then later they age out again from being able to talk and make money about what happened to them. They would age out again because they would get so old that nobody even cares or feels their story is relevant. So basically, you have a shelf life of a running back. You have a good five or six years that you can get your money back from the system. And it's not all about money. I'm sure none of them really care about the money. They all want to get their message out, but you can't get your message out when you live hand-to-mouth, or trashcan-hand-to-mouth in some scenarios.

I know some kids, and how they got a credit card is beyond me. But those credit cards are maxed out twice because they're out there doing the good work trying to get the message out about foster care. I, for instance, had already done my traveling for the year before a recent California trip came up. When I get to talk to kids I don't really care what you're paying me as long as there is something cool nearby that I can go and look at, or there are some people I want to advertise that I can go and talk to.

So, this last conference in California, not only was I only offered three hundred dollars in total, but when I explained to them I wouldn't be flying out because it wasn't cost effective and I don't do that, they didn't offer any more. So although, in six years I have never asked anybody for anything, this time I said I would go out and talk but I needed some more money to pay for it. I said if you send the money, I will donate magazine subscriptions in your name to underfunded child welfare agencies. They ended up sending about nine hundred dollars or whatever, just so I could get to where I needed to go. But I'm a big wheel in this thing and I get offered next to nothing.

For the last six years, I have seen hundreds of people become stars in the foster care advocacy world and then fade away, burn out before they should, whatever the causes. It is sad, but whenever a former foster kid says I'm going to be out talking and doing this stuff and I am going to write a book, I say books don't sell for foster care, they just don't. You get an occasional good one, a Kid Named Dirt or whatever that book was, or the other one where a millionaire adopted a kid that can block. I mean that's not par for the course. Outside of those, I am really hard pressed to think of any foster care related books that have sold anything.

Here's a catch-22, the people who are doing the most exploiting of former foster kids who want to speak out are the child welfare agencies themselves. I get invited to child welfare agency talks all the time. What they do is bring in hundreds of people from all over the country, and then those people have to pay for their room and board. They have to pay to go to the conference, they have to do all of that and then they have five hundred-dollar dinners each night. I went to one conference, it was the very first conference I'd ever been to and they fed everybody dinner. So, sushi comes out on a fish plate carved out of wood. Looking at the lady next to me, I said, "This is unbelievably wasteful." She asked, "What do you mean?" I responded, "All these people are coming here to learn about foster care and they just got fed what would be the equivalent of a years' worth of food at any child welfare agency. You can feed two hundred kids off this sushi platter. This is such a waste, and if I ever had a conference everybody would get peanut butter and jelly sandwiches. I would lower the cost of the conference and I would tell them to lower their expectations on food and that would be it."

Later, I was going up the escalator with another group of people and everybody was excited to have me there. It was my first time. The magazine had only been around for about six months and it was a hit right off the bat. They asked, have you met the president of the organization? I said I didn't think I had. They said she was coming on the escalator right now. I looked down and it was the lady I had talked to about how wasteful the food was! I walked up to her and told her I had no idea who she was during dinner and that I wouldn't have talked to her so plainly if I had known who she was. She told me to come back next year and I would see a difference. I came back the next year and they had peanut butter and jelly sandwiches. She walked up to me and told me she had an extra five thousand dollars just by not feeding everybody these luxury dinners. I told her that these people are civil service workers. They are used to not having much, so if you give them food, any kind of food, they will be happy. You could have come out here with a little bit of meat left on some chicken bones and they would have been excited.

So that was my introduction to this whole mess of public speaking on foster care. The one thing I see is that everybody is well-intentioned, but well-intentioned people make a lot of mistakes and they exploit people a lot of the times. They have so many blinders on that they can't notice that the kid who is coming to talk that day is probably only going to have that one meal today, and it is such a shame.

Everything upsets me about foster care. As far as the system as a whole, kids have to stop sleeping in offices. Agencies need to learn how to recruit foster parents better. Also, they regurgitate the same stuff every week. I just went to a human trafficking retreat in Chicago and no joke; they all said the same things they said at the human trafficking conference four years ago. No new information in the world of human trafficking, really? Then why aren't we trying harder to find new information? Why aren't we utilizing interviews to piece things together that we weren't sure of before? With everything that we do in foster care, there is such push back when it comes to change.

I live in a county full of crime. Well, I live adjacent to a county full of crime. The county I live in is quite poor. The county next to us has a city to deal with, suburbs to deal with. Caseworkers there have a caseload of under a hundred, whereas in the poor county that I live in, they have huge caseloads because they are snatching those kids up left and right because they're neglected. So, the preventative care over there keeps the kids out of foster care and keeps caseworker caseloads under a hundred, and the non-preventative care in my county has caseworkers with caseloads of like five hundred and they are significantly smaller areas. I mean tens of thousands of people less. That doesn't make any sense. So, when that happens you have to wonder why these people aren't talking to each other.

You don't need gimmicks in order to make this foster care thing work, you need proof, and you need feet on the ground. When we go to war in other countries we don't just shout from a distance, hey, stop that! We get in there and we have boots on the ground. We have people flying in. We attack it from all angles. But when they want to cut welfare, do they have all the stats they need? Where are our stats? Do you know how fast we update foster care numbers? I think every two or three years. It is always behind by two or three years. Luckily, this year somebody decided to pop the numbers together and do the best they could. We are at about four hundred and sixty-five thousand foster kids in the U.S., which is the highest since I started the magazine. It is the highest amount of kids that have been in care.

It can be frustrating coming from foster care. A lot of the times if you mention you were in foster care in any kind of work environment, your credibility goes down. I know CEOs who, like me, have GED's, but most of them had to get GED's because they were on drugs in high school. I aged out of foster care and didn't really have a choice but to get a GED. But, those others are not even frowned upon the same as someone who says they were in foster care.

You could say I murdered my cousin, and maybe that would be comparable to saying I was in foster care. The looks you get; the shift in the mood and everything. People think I'm charming and really enjoy me right away, but when they hear I was in foster care they start to look me over a little differently. Even when I meet people who don't know there is a foster care magazine will say, what do you do? I say, oh, I run a magazine. And they will respond, "Wow, that's awesome, you run a magazine. What's it about?" Once I say it's about foster care, it all changes. I hate that. That's my least favorite thing, and it has been happening since I was in foster care.

We don't need your sympathy. We need your action. I never needed anyone to feel bad for me. I needed them to tell me some of the basics, like how to wash my clothes. I needed them to tell me who not to talk to, or who to talk to. Unfortunately, that last one may not be quite true, because when you're in foster care you automatically learn who to trust and who not to trust for survival. I'm doubly dangerous because I used to sell cars, too. Not only can I tell you what kind of person you are, I could probably tell you your credit score too just by looking at you. That benefits you later in life, but when you tell people how you got that skill, it happens again, and they look down on you and there goes everything you worked for. So, it is a catch-22.

The thing that makes you different, unique, and special is also the thing that holds you back and makes people think that you're not different, unique, or special because they lump you into a bad category. You're categorized into this group because they saw a movie where a kid can play football so he made it out of foster care. They think every kid that is a little bit athletic can get out of foster care. I don't review any book or movie for the magazine where the parent turns out to be a millionaire because that is false hope they have been feeding us since Annie. Foster kids keep trying and hoping, and we keep thinking that it is meant to be great, but then you end up homeless anyway. I can't sing, and my hair is not red, so what am I supposed to do? This is turning into a rant session, but that is not my intent.

I don't normally tell people this in public, but there is not that much money in what I do. These are my problems. Anyway, I give a lot away, more than I really have. I have done that since I was in foster care. I remember there was another foster kid who came to my house in the wintertime, and the kid didn't have a coat. So, I gave him the only coat in the house, and it happened to be my best friend's coat. It was a big puffy coat and he loved it. He said he could walk through the neighborhood without having to feel dirty because it was a good coat; it was a nice off-the-rack thing. Now that I think about it, I hope he didn't get cut for it, because it was a really nice coat and he lived in a really bad area. I should have thought of that ahead of time I guess. This is the first time I have thought about the quality of the coat that I gave him and hope I didn't get him in trouble. They snatch stuff where I am from.

Over the years, I occasionally put out the word that I had no money so people would stop asking me so much for money. But, inevitably somebody came into hard times and they needed something. I told them I didn't have much, but they could have some. They could leave me a little, but they could have most of it. When someone is from care, they are very grateful for only about twenty minutes. But, then they go back to being concerned about how they are going to survive for the next two days, so I don't get upset.

I know there are lots of people who donate to help kids in foster care, and they don't understand why they are not considered saints. The God complex in foster care is a problem. Social workers think they are doing God's work. Maybe they are, but they don't have to act like they can walk on water. Also, there is some criticism because to some it seems only middle-aged white ladies and black churches are helping kids in foster care. It makes sense to be upset that more people aren't helping, but at the same time, what do you do? Tell one million well-intentioned, wealthy, middle-aged white ladies to not help? Where are you then? Black churches and white middle-aged ladies are exactly what keep foster care going, for good or for bad. So, to turn that money off and that volunteerism off would be detrimental to the system as a whole. These conflicting ideas are what I have to deal with all the time.

People come to me and think I have the answer that will fix everything in the foster care system. But, I'm a stupid goofball with a GED who picked the right product to sell. It really doesn't get bigger than that. I'm not deep, just as shallow as a pond. I have no depth to me. It's just that I want to make magazines, I want to make people laugh, and I want to make a little bit of money. That's all I really want out of life.

Kendra

Florida

I think I will start with the transition, the transition of going into foster care. I was probably eleven and did not know what a foster home was at all. There were some medical issues in my family; my mom had passed away when I was two. My aunt then took care of me, but she was ill and passed away when I was eleven. Other family members helped her take care of me. As my aunt became more ill and was close to passing away, they had social workers come to my school and pick me up. No one at home had given me any warning about it. Even though my family was not perfect, we were together. We went to family reunions. Even though my mom was not there, my other family members tried to help my aunt raise us.

I have three siblings, two sisters and one brother. We were pretty close growing up and we did a lot of things together. We lived with my aunt, but my other family members came to help and I had a Godmother who helped, as well. When my aunt knew she was going to be passing soon she decided to make this decision, but did not talk about it. No one talked about it to me. When I went to school and these people showed up at school, they just told me I was going with them. I was confused. I went to a foster home in Miami Gardens, and I did not know what a foster home was. I saw a lady and I saw all these teenage girls that looked like me. I did not really know what was going on. The social worker had not explained in the car what was really going on. It took me a while to figure it all out. Ultimately, I could still visit my grandparents; they just did not have the ability to take care of me. That was very traumatic for me, very traumatic.

I went from being an A student, a focused student, to being a student who just did not care. I was in a new middle school and basically slacked the whole year. The teachers there did not know this was not what I was normally like. They did not know I was acting out because of a situation that had just occurred. I did not receive any counseling around that time that I can remember. Much earlier, I did get counseling when my mom had passed away. When I was really young, I remember receiving counseling for that situation, but that was also very traumatic. I was still involved with my grandparents; they just did not have the ability to take care of me.

What eventually changed my outlook on things was when I moved to a foster home down south. It was run by a lady who was more of a parent. She wanted me to do well in school. She rewarded me for doing well in school. She set her expectations high and I started to do better. I actually came out of my depression. Then I had a teacher who saw I was a little bit behind in math and she helped me. She saw I was smart, but had missed a few steps because I had not been paying attention in the prior grade.

She was a sort of mentor to me and helped me catch up. I ended up winning the highest math award that year. I was very happy about that.

Then I began to pick up my studies from there. As I went into high school, I started to run track and do things like that because I wanted to do more. That foster mom, she was a really good foster mom. I had stayed in about six homes and I cannot say that about all of them, but that one, she and her husband were really good. I left their house when I was about sixteen or seventeen, teenage rebellion, and I moved into another foster home in the city where I was from. There I worked at a local supermarket while in high school, and I was also running track and volunteering. Because of all the things I was doing, I won a trip to London through the police department. I was blessed to able to go to London.

I was doing a program where you get work while you are in high school. So, I did that at a supermarket. I loved my coworkers. I loved going to work. I loved doing that. But this is the thing, the reason I started working was because when I moved to that foster home, the foster mom said no one could stay with her in the house from seven a.m. to seven p.m. on Saturdays and Sundays. So, I thought if I couldn't be there all day on weekends, then I had to be doing something during that time. So, I decided I was going to get a job.

I got the job almost immediately after moving into that foster home. After a while the foster mom got to know me and said I did not need to leave during the weekend days but everyone else had to. She said I could act like I was leaving and then come right back. So that was one of the things she did that I liked, but one of the things she did that I did not like was that she did not give me my allowance. Many of the foster parents I had did not give me an allowance, but they did give me everything I needed and more, like toiletries and things you need. But this lady did not give us the things we needed, and she did not give us the money we were supposed to receive.

I had started going to a youth group of current and former foster kids, and they said I should be getting an allowance as part of foster care. They told us what our rights were as foster kids. So, I learned that I was supposed to be getting an allowance. I had been wondering why we were not getting money because we needed things. I was working, so I had some things, but some of the other girls in the house stole them because they were basic things you need, like underwear, toothpaste, hair supplies and things like that. I was getting upset that they were stealing my stuff, but I also did not know how they were going to get these basic supplies. From a man? Where else were they going to get them from?

Then my case worker came to see me and asked if there was anything I needed. She asked if I was okay, and what was going on. I told her that I was okay because I was working, but there were some girls in the house who were not okay because they did not have the basic things and we were not getting an allowance. She said she would tell the lady we were supposed to be getting an allowance. I told her I did not want her to say anything because I did not want to move again. I was in twelfth grade and about to graduate, and I was getting ready to go to college. I did not want to move to another house. She said she would just act like it was on her talking points when she spoke with the foster mom. So when she came over to the house to do the monthly visit, she had her checklist when she was talking with the foster mom. She went down the list of questions. When was the last time Kendra went to the doctor? How is school going for Kendra? How much is Kendra currently getting for allowance? When she mentioned the allowance, the lady was like, what? I do not give anyone an allowance. The social worker then told her she was required to give fifty-five dollars a month so they could buy things for themselves. That should be given to Kendra and the others. The lady said okay, and from that day on she gave all the girls in the house their allowance to buy those things for themselves. So that was really good.

After all of that, I ended up going to college. I had known from the second grade that I wanted to go to college. I knew, because I was in a program in the inner city of Miami, in, you know, rough neighborhoods where kids have big, big dreams but they also have a lot of violence and other obstacles that make it challenging to reach those dreams. So, the program staff came to my school and told the parents that if their child stays with them in their program and makes it to college, they would pay for them to go to college. That was the promise they made. They wanted to help if you stayed with them. We signed a contract saying we were going to stay with them, and we were going to succeed and go from there.

With that program, we went to extracurricular activities. I started it while I was still with my family and continued with it from second to sixth grade even after I went into foster care. They had a mentoring program. One man, Ricky, was our project coordinator. Ricky would mentor us and call our parents. He was like a father to me and is still like a father to me all these years later. He just really stayed with us, motivated us and encouraged us.

I was in that program and that was where I got the idea that I wanted to go to college. I wanted something other than what I saw around me. I never knew what I wanted to be when I grew up, but I knew I wanted something more. My daughter, she knows what she wants to be when she grows up. But I did not know exactly what I wanted to do. I just knew I wanted to help people. That was my only goal. I wanted to do something where I could help people. So that program planted a seed that my goal was a possibility. So even with all of the things I went through, I knew that college was my end result. I knew I was going and I started to prepare for college.

Then I found another organization that focused on education opportunities. It was around the same time I was working at the supermarket, I met my mentor, Karen, through this new organization. This was one of those organizations that believed in independence through education. They believe in helping foster kids truly become independent through education and employability skills. I believe they got started in South Africa helping with education and building schools. Then they came to the United States and saw there were laws that allowed foster kids to go to college for free. Around that time, a lot of foster kids did not know they could go to college for free. There is basically a statute in Florida that waives the costs of college until you are twenty-eight. So, when this organization found out about this benefit for foster kids, they decided to educate the kids about it. When they told me about it I thought it was extra help for me so I could become independent. They had an independent living stipend that gives financial assistance so foster kids do not need to work so much while getting their education. They gave me that stipend, but they also provided me with a mentor; Karen.

Karen basically followed up with me on my dreams and goals. She would say, did you take your SAT? Did you schedule it? Did you talk with your advisor? She was just checking to see that I was hitting the benchmarks I wanted to hit. She was a great person to me, and very, very encouraging. I decided I wanted to do a college tour. I was making five dollars and twenty-five cents an hour at the supermarket, and I do not know if it was two paychecks or one, but the college tour was around two hundred and fifty dollars. I was in Tallahassee for about four days. I got to the campus and I loved it. I loved that there were so many, I am going to say this, African American men and women doing great and positive things. I had never seen that before. A whole campus of everyone doing great things and I loved it. I decided this was where I wanted to go. This was where I wanted to be.

When I got back I knew where I wanted to go, and I finished the application process. I finished everything I needed to do, my testing, my application and everything. The next question was, who was going to take me to orientation? This is an issue for a lot of foster youth because they require you to have a parent at orientation. I was used to doing everything for myself, but they required me to have a parent there.

The one foster parent I liked so much, the one that was so amazing who helped me get my grades up, ended up passing around that time. I went to her funeral and people there asked me how I was going to get to college and go to orientation. Who was going to take me? I told them I really did not know since this foster mom had passed. I did not have anyone to take me. They said I should ask her husband since he had been my foster father. So I asked him if he would take me and he said yes. His sister had a house near the college so we would not need to pay for a hotel. He rented a car and took me to my orientation. He had his own business, so he could have been doing other things that weekend. He even took me back the following weekend for me to start college. He spent maybe three days there to make sure I settled in okay.

When we got to the college I realized I did not have food. I had the meal plan, but you still need little snacks in your room. So, he took me to the store and bought food and any other little things I needed. It was three hundred dollars' worth of stuff. He had not been my foster parent in years, but he bought all of that and carried everything up to my room. He was there to sign papers with me. You would not have been able to tell he was not my parent.

I had other support too. The police department in my county bought my refrigerator and microwave, and things like that. They also gave me paper, binders and pens, everything I would need. My mentor, Karen, got my laptop and printer. Then my foster dad's sister, the one who had the house near the college, bought my trunk and some decorations from the department store for my room. Just thinking about how many people helped me, I realize how blessed I was. It was like a community effort. I really enjoyed my experience in college.

The biggest thing I will say about foster kids who face so many challenges is they need to know early on that college is an option. They need to start preparing early for when they leave the foster care system and the support stops. They need to be ready to earn a living. While in the system, say they are in independent living, they will receive about twelve hundred dollars a month or something like that. But that will end, and they should be focusing early on college or learning a trade so they can support themselves when the time comes. An issue that foster kids face is that they do not have a support system. We do not have a lot of people, like regular parents, to support us when something goes wrong. My daughter has me. When my daughter graduates from college and maybe something happens, she will not be outside and homeless because I will be there for her as her backbone. I am there for her, but when a foster child is on their own and something happens, they likely do not have that support. They may start living from couch to couch, or on the floor and eventually maybe outside and homeless. It can be hard.

For example, with me, I was college educated and I still experienced various issues. I have been homeless before. Just one little thing can do it. I made good money, but my car was stolen and I ended up spending about three thousand dollars on rental car fees. That caused some hardship for me. Little things that come up can end up causing significant hardship, and if you do not have a support system it can be devastating for you.

Another thing that is important for foster kids is counseling. I've had to fight a lot as an adult, and am still fighting, to not let certain issues affect me. When you move from home to home to home over your whole childhood, you get this runaway mentality. It can cause you to back away every time you get in a new situation, to think that it is not going to work out. You just start thinking about where you are going to next. This also causes issues with trust. It causes issues with a lot of things. So, I think that I probably should have had some counseling back then, and I think that a lot of the foster youth would benefit from some counseling. Even if there are not any red flags, they may benefit from counseling because those transitions in foster care are not normal. Normal kids do not go from home to home, and six schools before they even get to high school. I then went to five high schools. So, they need to get used to being somewhere and going somewhere else and getting used to that, and then yet again going somewhere else and getting used to that.

People helped me, and they helped my daughter, so I am very thankful. I had help getting to college from my foster parent, but even after college when I moved back to Miami and got my master's degree many people helped me. I currently work as a professor at a college. I teach accounting at the college and am very sought out as a professor. I also work for the county as a compliance auditor. I am still trying to grow as a twenty-nine-year-old, and people help me along the way financially, spiritually and mentally, and I really appreciate that. The story I've told you here speaks to some of the struggles I had to endure, but it was also about the outcome I was able to achieve. It is not just about graduating from college or getting a master's degree, it is about raising my daughter, who is a very talented young lady. It's about gaining full employment instead of being underemployed. It is about being a professor as well as an auditor. I am proud of my accomplishments and just so thankful for all of those people who helped me along the way. Overall, there are some good foster homes and there are some good people, and there are some people who need a little more training or a little more compassion. For me, it worked out for my good. I met a lot of great people. I will say that I have seen God's love through people.

Christine

Washington, D.C.

I recently got my bachelor's in social work and am currently enrolled in the mental health counseling master's program. I now work with young adults who recently exited the foster care system. My dad died when I was four, and Mom died when I was ten. At the time my mother died I had already been in foster care for six years, but it wasn't until she died that I was separated from my sisters. My mother ended up calling social services when I was four because she had a drug addiction. I will always remember the words she said to us, "It's not because I don't love you; it's because I want a better life for you." So I always remembered those words and that she cared, even when I was angry and had to be split from my sisters.

I came into the foster care system when I was four. It wasn't a typical set up, because I had a bond with my mother. Even though I was in foster care, I saw her every weekend. But then she got sick with HIV and had kidney failure. My foster mother would leave all four kids with my mom for long periods, even though she was sick and weak.

One day my mother and my foster parent got into it and hurtful words were said. At that point my mother had been clean and off drugs, she was just sick. After that conversation my mother went home and we never heard from her again. You don't tell someone who is sick that they will never see their kids again. She relapsed, and it killed her.

This caused me to react. I was ten years old, and yes, I had behavioral problems. I hadn't been fully utilizing therapy. When I originally went to behavior modification therapy my foster parent would say don't share anything with the therapist, don't tell her anything that is going on in this house, so I didn't. I'd sit there for a whole hour not saying anything at all. I was doing my art therapy, but she put me on all these medicines. Instead of getting to the root of my problems and figuring out why I was acting like that, she said I had ADHD, a learning disability, and was emotionally disturbed.

I got tired of being treated like people thought I was just like my mother. After my mom died, I started talking to my therapist and would look forward to therapy sessions. I started to self-advocate. I needed more. I was still dealing with foster home issues, even though she helped me with my mom issue. I was still going to these foster homes, and each home was a story. I was in seven foster homes and two group homes.

There are a lot of kids in the foster care system that don't get the help they need. That's why I'm passionate about what I'm doing. I got my bachelors in social work and I work with homeless families. At first I wanted to do social work, but once I started getting into it, I needed to go to the larger system. Now I want to be involved with laws and policies. Some systems are set up for people to be failures. In my current work, the goal is to help people become self-sufficient with employment, education and their mental health being treated. I agree with that approach. If kids go through these different systems with different approaches, it's hard for them. They are used to people referring them here and there, and they are used to people not being able to help them and just backing away because of it. Kids expect you to back away because they've seen it so much. I'm the complete opposite. I'm going to be in your face to help you until you get tired of me. I'm sorry; I'm jumping all over the place.

My fourth home was very structured and that helped me change a lot of my ways. She cleaned for a living, celebrities and wealthy people's houses and she made me clean for an allowance. She taught me how to work for money, not just to expect it. I could have been adopted by her, but I said no because she was just so strict. But her house was the one where I was able to get off my medicine. Also, the majority of foster parents never gave me money, but she did. I didn't realize until I stayed with her that they were supposed to give me money.

When I came to her house I was at a behavior modification school, but they were teaching us all at the same level. I had been doing my art therapy and I was ready for more. I thought, if they didn't teach to my level, then I needed to go back to regular school. I advocated for myself and my foster mother advocated for me to go back to public school. At that point, I hadn't seen my social worker for a month, so I didn't have medicine for a month and was doing fine. The foster mom said, "You didn't need medicine, you just needed Jesus. You just needed some structure." Then she reached out to the social worker and the social worker agreed, and we talked about my improvements. My therapist had known me since I was six, and she had mixed feelings about whether I was ready for public school. But I knew I had more potential than that behavior modification school and I didn't want to graduate with nine people. I was ready to move on. I was utilizing the services.

So, I did end up in public school. I went to different high schools each year because I was moving foster homes. My social worker felt I needed an Individualized Education Plan or IEP to take advantage of this or that program, but the schools said I was fine. They said I was doing well and on point, nothing was wrong with me. I was on the right level. They threw out the IEP. Also, the Rehabilitation Services Administration rejected me because they said I didn't have any disabilities. I already knew this.

Along the way in foster care I got linked to a few mentor programs with events to interact with mentors. So I was going to those, and then I had my own mentor. There was so much to help me cope with my mother's death. Before my mother died, I decided I wanted to be adopted and she was the only one supporting me on it at that time. Everybody else was asking me why I would want to be adopted. I went on TV with a program that looks for adoptive families, and I got about ninety families that called. I settled for the third family and was in the process of getting adopted, but of course it didn't work. So I went back into the foster care system and went back on TV looking for a family, and still went to the mentoring events.

My social worker told me I needed to be with this rich woman who expressed an interest in adopting me. She was a model from Europe. My social worker thought that she had this great set up for me. But I had only one question for this rich woman and she couldn't answer it. When I asked her when I could see my sisters, she had no answer. I didn't want to be rich so I told my social worker no, and she called me dumb for not choosing to be with her. I wanted a family, but I didn't want to settle for just anybody. Moving forward I went from home to home.

My last home was perfect, it was a two-parent home and four kids, and it worked out. It was nice. I never really had any problems there. So I asked the parents if they wanted to adopt me. You can ask anyone you are connected to, to adopt you or have guardianship. Unfortunately, they said no. I was eighteen at the time and it was very discouraging. The head of one of the mentoring programs I was in told me I still had a chance to be adopted. She said she still had faith.

Over the next two years, I decided that if this foster family wasn't going to adopt me there was no point in them getting paid to keep me. So I advocated for myself to be in an independent living program, which is where older kids in foster care receive benefits to live independently with another older foster kid as a roommate. When I moved into independent living my mentor had moved back to New Jersey, to her hometown, but we were still in contact. Ever since I was thirteen, my mentor was always there for me. So she called me and said she needed to ask me something. She asked if it was okay to adopt me. The first thing I said was yes. I didn't care if I was twenty. I had been through the system in all types of homes where they didn't care, and I felt I just wanted a family. Of course, some people had something negative to say about it, but I didn't care. My mentor and I agreed that I'd stay in independent living and I would age out of the system. This meant we would wait to do the adoption until I turned twenty-one. So, we went to the court when I was twenty-one and it became permanent and it was finalized. She asked if I wanted to go to New Jersey to live with her, but I had started college so wanted to stay down in D.C. Also, I had to make sure my sisters stayed together. I was tired of starting over and I knew I could visit her in New Jersey.

I was going to college and in my second year ended up meeting a boy and we were helping each other out. I ended up staying with him and got pregnant. Many people told me I was not going to be able to finish school. But my mentor and now adoptive mom said, "If you think you can do it; do it. It's your decision and I will support you." So, it was my last year of college, I was pregnant, and I had to think through a way to do it. I decided to take two classes in the spring and two in the summer. I started working security and did whatever I had to do, and I finally graduated. It was a struggle, but I always remembered my mother's words and I didn't want to repeat history. My mindset was to just keep going, because I remembered my experiences growing up. I'm also glad

I had the support of my mentor because once I had the baby I was still able to go to school. I would bring my baby, Christian, with me. Everyone at college knew Christian and he was very popular.

When I finish what I need to do here, maybe I can move up to New Jersey to be near my adoptive mom. I wanted to be adopted because I needed that family support. I had been through a lot of hard times. I speak to my adoptive mom often and try to see her at least once a month. I go up to New Jersey and am thankful for her support. I try not to ask her for things; I guess it is my pride.

If I have a general message for people, it is that the foster care system has to change. Working with the kids in foster care as I do now, I say we need to hold them accountable for their actions, they need structure. I let them know it will take a team, but that they need to want to change too. I keep moving forward, and I have to be part of that change. To adoptive parents, I say don't give up on a child. They are misunderstood. Therapy is the key. Also, social workers need to put in more effort and get to the root of the problems. All these kids want is support and someone to talk with even if they don't show it. I tell the kids I work with that I have been where you have been, and I'm not going to give up. Some of the kids like me and others don't, but I'm going to go above and beyond my job for all of them.

Sarah

Montana

I have been working with kids in foster care since high school. My first experience was volunteering in a child abuse and neglect shelter, an emergency shelter where I grew up in Minnesota. I did that my senior year in high school after volunteering previous years with terminally ill children in the hospital. I really liked volunteering with terminally ill children, but then I had this opportunity to do a different volunteer placement at this child abuse and neglect shelter. Once I got there, I realized these kids are so much more profoundly impacted by what has happened to them than children who have a terminal illness. I still saw hope and joy in the terminally ill children, and then I started working with these kids in the shelter and there was just a lack of hope and not very much joy.

I'd always wanted to work with kids, and I thought I was going to be a child life specialist at a children's hospital. I don't know if you've ever heard of that position, but they run these play rooms that help the kids sort of adjust to their hospitalization and be less nervous. They can play with medical supplies before they have surgery, or they can put on the mask and dress up so it's not so intimidating. I thought that was what I was going to do, but after I finished that year volunteering, I really wanted to focus more on kids who have been victims of abuse or neglect and were in the child welfare system. So I went to college and got my degree in social work.

I went to undergraduate school at the university here. I wanted to stay in Montana, so I began working at a group home for four adolescent boys, an intensive-level therapeutic group home for boys who are either in the child welfare system or the juvenile justice system, but mostly child welfare. I did that for a couple of years and was sort of frustrated with the system. So I started thinking about what I could do next.

I applied for law school and ended up at school in Denver where they had a children's advocacy center as part of their program. That was a year-long clinic where you represented kids, parents and whatnot, but it was a multidisciplinary sort of model with a team. I did that model of representation within the child welfare system, working part-time at the center while I went to law school full-time. I eventually switched to part-time in law school while working at the center. I did that for three years with a pediatric attorney, doctors and social workers. They're co-located with the medical school's pediatric department and the local hospital there. I got to do a ton of work in the field of child abuse prevention and treatment while I was in law school. But we wanted to come back to Montana afterward and settle.

After I got my law degree, I started working back in Montana as a Deputy County Attorney representing the state in child abuse and neglect civil cases. I did some criminal cases, but mostly civil.

I did that for about three and a half years. I then represented the state in district court for about seven and half years before moving to the Attorney General's Office. There, I was an Assistant Attorney General and did civil and criminal child abuse and neglect cases in seventeen counties in Montana.

I was then talked into leaving the practice of law to go into administration. First, I was the Program Bureau Chief for the Child and Family Services Division, which is the state agency in Montana that does all the child protection services, child welfare I guess you could call it. So, I started with that agency as their Program Bureau Chief. Then the director, also called the Division Administrator in our state system, left, so I was hired into that position. I was the administrator of Montana's child protection system for five years when I'd had enough and decided to go back into practicing law. Since then, for the last year or so, I have had a private practice part-time, and I've done work for the Office of the Public Defender taking conflict cases where I represent children and parents in child abuse and neglect cases. I like doing both. So at this point in my career I have been a social worker, a lawyer for the state, a lawyer for kids and their parents and, obviously, an administrator for the state. I feel like I've seen the system from just about every possible point of view.

I have worked with kids of all ages. The kids in my case load right now are everywhere from one year old to almost eighteen. I would say that right now I am pretty happy being back in the court system rather than in the administrative side. I think one of the hardest things for me, in terms of that position, was just the level of bureaucracy the system has. It feels like, over time, there have been more and more layers of federal regulations and federal laws stacked on top of state laws. Because you know, family law is very state driven, so except for the child welfare funding that comes through the federal laws, you have this whole set of state statutes. Every state looks very different, and you have to superimpose those federal requirements on the state ones as well as the policies and procedures and all of that. In my old job it felt like my focus was more on compliance than on actually helping kids. I really felt like I never got to spend time with kids, or talk to kids, or parents. I enjoy both sides just as much, because I think kids really need their parents, or some parent, whether that is their biological parents or, if that doesn't work, adoptive parents.

Based on all my many years of experience and all the different caps I've worn, I think it is most important that every child has significant relationships in their lives that are there for them no matter what, no matter when. Sadly, I've seen a lot of cases where adoptions didn't work out and the kids have come back into the system. I don't know, it makes me a bit skeptical sometimes about what the federal definition of permanency is. In the federal view, when a child has been adopted, the child has now achieved permanency. This means something and affects funding. For me, it is more about the relationship the child has with that person and whether or not that's permanent. To me, as a lawyer, all that adoption really is in the sense of the law is a piece of paper, and it can be undone. It is more important on a personal level that kids find a real connection. So I felt like my old job was not really about that. It was about federal reviews and legislative audits and how many days overdue your reports are.

I also see it's a field that is generally not well-funded. I can only speak for Montana, but I know that our case workers carry excessively high caseloads. There has always been high turnover in the front-line positions. There has always been a struggle to fill those positions. I see that now, even in my cases, the workers will change. The workers will be really new, and won't really understand the totality of their jobs, or of the legal system, or any of that. I think that is obviously a huge detriment to the kids, and the families who are looking to the system to help. I mean, sometimes it can create a good outcome and a good life course for them, but I don't think that happens as much as it should, at all. I think for the country, it's time we reconsider the whole approach we have to child welfare. There are two types of federal funding, one is more focused on prevention and is meant to preserve safe and stable families, and the other type is for foster care which is after the children have been removed from their homes. The amount of money Montana receives in these types of funding is completely out of whack. Like one million for the prevention side, sixteen million or whatever for the foster care side.

I think until the resources are sort of aligned to get to families earlier, the child welfare system is going to continue to spiral out of control. The attempts to just further regulate it seem, in my mind, to be a big backward step. I'm happily not in charge of Montana's next federal child and family services review. Unless it's changed, I have yet to hear of a state that passed one of these reviews, so it's really not a very positive process. In my old administrator job, I was always in a position where people were questioning why our agency was not doing better. They would say they were going to take resources away until we could prove we used the resources in a more effective manner. In the end, this approach just hurts kids.

So I finally got to a point where I felt like I was not even part of any solution, and maybe more part of a problem. At least when I go to court now, it is one kid, one case and you feel like you can affect the outcome for that kid in that case. Maybe not in every case does it go exactly how you hope, but there is a lot more of a feeling that you have a direct role in the decision making. And I get to talk to kids a lot and I really like that. I don't know, I just worry that our country is going in the wrong direction.

Some of the work I did at that center when I was in law school involved being exposed to what is called the nurse family partnership model of home visiting, where a nurse works one-on-one with the pregnant woman to improve prenatal and child rearing practices through the child's second birthday. Home visiting is one of the interventions that shows some of the best evidence in terms of the prevention of child abuse and neglect. I know there are some federal funds going to some of the evidence-based home visiting models. I think that is a positive step, but at least in our state that funding really isn't tied to child welfare, and it really isn't directed to at-risk families. It's all just voluntary versus I guess what should be a universal requirement. I don't know, I think we have this assumption that parents just know what to do when they have a kid and that is so far from the truth. I like to say, you know, there is a test you have to take before you can drive, and you have to go prove you're worthy of a fishing license, but anyone can have a child. I'm not opposed to that, but what I am opposed to is that we seem to presume that if you have a child you know what to do, and we don't offer people services. Like just letting them know it's really going to be hard, maybe not all the time, but at least some of the time it's going to be the hardest job you have ever had.

It is hard for anybody, but we presume people know what to do. You know, I have two kids, one with special needs. I was an educated new mom who didn't have my kids until I was in my thirties. I remember my littlest one who was born with Downs being in the neonatal intensive care unit or NICU, and I was getting ready to discharge. She'd been in there about ten days, and I asked when I would get my public health nurse visitor. The nurse said, oh, well we just marked that you don't want one. I said, well, I do want one. They thought I wouldn't need one. So even that attitude is probably more pervasive, that people just don't think that we should offer parents help, that somehow that's offensive. So, I don't know. I really, really, really have worked with enough kids to know that most, if not all, love their biological family and their parents. And regardless of what the biological family has done, or how long it's been since the kids have seen them, the kids still feel a connection. So, why we don't invest more in that connection and making those relationships positive is beyond me.

I just can't get over the fact that we think we are helping kids by taking them out of the place they feel the safest, even though it might not seem safe. It's emotionally safer in so many ways than foster care. When you look at the studies, you realize that the emotional stress and all the trauma of the system is just as unhealthy for children in the long run, as getting hit or watching someone in your home get hit. I worry that we aren't putting the resources where they might make the most difference in the next generation. I worry because we aren't one of those countries that provide a universal home visit or a public health nurse while the child is little in order to support those parents. And we don't provide child care. I mean, we expect parents to work, and we particularly expect lower income parents to work. We have that conversation a lot in our legislature, that people need to be working, these people we serve in some of these systems. Yet we don't have affordable child care.

In Montana we have a dire shortage of child care, particularly for infants. We don't have a place for our parents to send their children when they have to work. So, we see a lot of bad cases with physical abuse by a boyfriend, or by a caregiver, just because a mom didn't have the resources to find someone to take care of her child so she could work, so she could meet her kid's needs. I see those resources getting cut. I don't see us supporting those parents. We don't provide a lot of healthcare or child care; all of those things will make a difference to a family. As long as we continue to have families without that support, I just think we're going to see more and more children who are coming into the child welfare system. At least in Montana, our numbers have gone up. We're not one of those states that saw any sort of reduction in foster care. We've also seen a ton of methamphetamine use, tons of opiates, and a ton of neonatal abstinence syndrome. In some areas of our state hospitals say over half of our babies are born addicted to substances.

So now that I'm on the flip side, I get to represent some of these moms. I'll hear there wasn't treatment available before the children were removed from the home, but once the department gets involved and the children are removed they will pay for these services. This is because of the way Montana receives the federal funding, not much for prevention. A lot of times you see the parents take the services and do a really good job, and the kids go home. I always think to myself, well why did it take getting to a crisis to get services? I can tell you, this mother has been asking for help the whole time, but we are only going to give it to her once we've taken the children out of the home.

I don't know, I'm happy to be doing my cases again and not trying to work on the system level. Everything people seem to be doing at the system level seems, in my mind, to be just like a bandage instead of addressing the problems. I have spent a lot of time with a lot of kids who are not yet in the child welfare system. I do guardian ad litem work in civil cases where there are some concerns in the home, but the children haven't been removed, and I can tell you that their lives aren't perfect either. Had someone made that call to child services at some point, they may have ended up in foster care. Yet all of these kids seem to do much better than kids in the system, even in those environments. It just doesn't seem to reach nearly the level of what I see with a kid who's been removed for something similar and now made their way through the system.

I had a foster care case in the past year, an older youth, and I think she was in eight placements, eight treatment facilities in a year with no resolution. She has a father who has not been able to parent because he is incarcerated, and a deceased mother, so she had been staying with a relative. I just wonder, had the Department not removed her from the relative's home, she probably would have done better even though they were struggling. She has since been in eight different treatment facilities where she's been put on a million medications. And so, you know, we can go to court, and we can ask the judge to order them to find her a lower level placement, meaning a foster home instead of a treatment facility. We could also research relatives for a potential placement and all that, but if the social worker has fifty cases and fifty kids, all of whom need immediate attention it just takes too much for it to get done. So, I feel like it's gotten to the point in the system where everyone is just so overwhelmed, that it's hard to do good work, at least on all of your cases.

I still haven't lost hope. I feel like I left my last job with very little hope, and now that I get to spend more time with kids and see some cases where things go really well, I have more hope. We just closed a case a couple of weeks ago where reunification occurred, and I represented the mom. She was just amazing, she did a great job and her child was so happy to be home. So those are the cases that make me think, yeah, I did make this work. So, I feel like I'm back in a better spot, but I can't imagine being one of those kids in the system in a bad spot. If I felt hopeless as an administrator, I can't even imagine how they must feel. It's probably not even in the same universe of feeling.

North Carolina

It was just never easy, you know, being in foster care. We lived in New Jersey, and there were problems in the home and I would stay with neighbors for long periods. I actually thought for a long time that in this early period of my life I was in foster care, but I subsequently learned that no, I was just staying with others for long periods. Eventually people got tired of it and, on one occasion, I was with folks for just too long. So they called child welfare, and I ended up in the foster care system.

One of my family members always stayed in contact with me while I was in foster care. We had a good relationship with him, but he would always tell me to just be good for my foster parents. I would see him every birthday, on Easter, before school started at the end of summer, and I would see him at Christmas. He would take me shopping and we had dinner or lunch, or I would do something else with him, but that was the extent of it. I never stayed at his home. He never did any full-time parenting.

Some years ago, I decided to write to the New Jersey government to get my foster care records. They responded with a written summary of my history, since they do not send the actual records. It showed that at five years old I went into foster care. Then I literally bounced around different foster homes for what seemed like a lifetime. We lived in all kinds of conditions. By nine, I was settled into one foster home that ended up being the one I emancipated from. Of course, the system then was not what it is today. Today, foster parents are clearly instructed there is to be no physical discipline. Foster children often suffer from trauma; maybe they were physically abused in their own home, so you do not want to traumatize them even more. Well, back then foster parents were not trained that way. I had regular beatings in some of those foster homes.

There was also food deprivation. I remember times when the biological family would eat and we would only get to eat whatever was left over. There were also times when we did not get to eat at all. So we would take food and hide it for later, just to make sure we had food in case we did not get another meal. I did not know what hoarding was at the time, but I look back now and understand that we were hoarding because we were not given enough food and did not know when our next meal would be.

With one foster family, while they lived in a home with a roof and running water, they made the foster kids live next to them in a house they were building. It was just the frame for a house with an outhouse, no roof or running water. I remember that because I remember being afraid to go into the outhouse. This family had a lot of foster kids they kept in that unfinished house, and I remember we called each other brother and sister. I was moved out of that home once the agency, I guess, found out that I was not actually being cared for in a home.

In those foster homes where there was physical abuse, food deprivation or other problems, I was really afraid to tell the social worker what was going on, and back then there was really no opportunity for us to do so. It seems that today social workers are trained to spend some alone time with the kids so that they can find out how they are doing and what is going on in the home. There are also guardian ad litems now that they did not have before, who are people the court appoints to investigate what is in the best interests of a child. Also, there are Court Appointed Special Advocates or CASAs today who are another set of eyes and ears on behalf of the children. I did not have any of that. A social worker would only come periodically, and in all honesty, we would only see the social workers when they would come to move us. Once we settled into the home, we would see our social worker very infrequently.

The reality of that kind of life and the bouncing around from home to home is that people were, frankly, just in it for the money. I did not have loving, encouraging people taking care of me. They did not tell me I was okay and that I was capable of doing things. So my self-confidence suffered. To this day I kind of question everything. Unfortunately, for me and for a lot of people who were raised in foster care, we grew up without a lot of people really encouraging us, telling us that we are good and telling us we can accomplish things. So, I never really developed that confidence and belief in myself. I am always questioning things. I am never really comfortable in my skin. Even after graduating from high school, college and then law school, I just never felt like I was good enough. I never felt like I did enough. If I did something good, I would give the credit to other people. I would say that I was able to do that because this person helped me, or that person helped me. So, building self-esteem and encouraging young people who are in foster care is just so, so critical. I always felt like there was something wrong with me because I felt my mother did not want me, and because of how I was treated in those foster homes.

I suffered through those different environments and mistreatments, and if you feel your whole family does not love you, especially your parents, then you think, why should anyone else? Why should anyone love me? Why should anyone care about me? So, I went through childhood feeling that way. I only ended up going to college because of my home economics teacher. I was not the best kid in school. I spent a fair amount of time visiting the principal's office or sitting in detention because I was just stubborn and acting out. If it was not something I wanted to do, I did not do it. I just felt miserable in my own skin, and I wanted everyone else to be miserable too.

In one school, we had to take certain courses like home economics. So, I took it, but I would go into class and put my head down on the desk. If the teacher asked me to do something, I said no. I did not want to be bothered. One day after class she told me she would not have this. She said I could not behave this way. This is a fun class. We cook. We eat. We have fun. We laugh, you know, what is your problem? What is up with you? Eventually, I told her how miserable my life had been, how miserable I felt. I did not feel there was anything to feel good about with eating and cooking. She responded that this was not going to be my life forever. She told me I really needed to take care of myself and get an education. That is how you make a difference for yourself. So she said she was not going to tolerate my behavior in her class and that she would be checking on me in my other classes. She was a person who told me I could go to college, and eventually was the one who started looking at colleges with me. She helped me complete all of the paperwork. I told her I did not have money to go to college and that I did not have parents to pay for it. She helped me find a program that helped minority students get into college and pay for it. She helped me complete that application and I ended up going to a university in New Jersey, all because of her encouragement.

Because of her, I thought I wanted to be a teacher. But in

college we had to do a semester of student teaching to get the certification and I realized I did not have the skills it takes to work with kids like that. I learned I was not so good with that. So, when I graduated I moved back to the area where I grew up and took a job as a community outreach coordinator in the state's legal services office. The lawyers did the legal work, but that was a time in the seventies when legal services programs were being cut, funding was being cut, and so they were looking at ways they could still deliver services to the community but reduce the number of lawyers. That was my job for a number of years, and there were some really positive influences there. There were people who would encourage me, but I still had a lot of self-doubt. I did not think about going to law school, but really admired those lawyers. You know; real public servants. They deeply cared about people.

I eventually left that organization because of additional funding cuts and took a job at an airline startup with good pay, stock options, travel benefits and great opportunities. I worked there for about five years. While there, I worked with a young woman who was going to law school full-time and still working full-time for the airline. I thought, wow, she is an incredible person. I wished I could be like her. I talked with her a little bit about my past and what I thought I wanted to do, and that I had been encouraged by the lawyers I worked with before by what they did. She told me I should go to law school, so eventually I did apply and got into a couple of schools. I went to law school in New Jersey, and there were more positive influences there. I met so many people doing so many things, and I thought maybe I could do them too. I was still not as confident as I should be, as it was ingrained in me to be worried about what the future might hold. Toward the end of law school I applied to clerkships and I was fortunate enough to get to be a law clerk for a judge in Washington, D.C. Much like my home economics teacher, he was such a good mentor. He was so encouraging, telling me I could do things. I did not tell him about my history in foster care. One thing about being in foster care is you get pretty guarded about who you tell about it. I always felt like if people knew I grew up in foster care, they would not like me. You know, even my own family did not like me, so I felt I could not share that.

This made some conversations a little awkward. This judge I clerked with would talk about how his dad was a police officer and that his mom was an awesome woman. I did not have those kinds of stories to tell. No Sunday dinners with grandma and all the family coming together. No wonderful aunts and uncles. I just did not have them. But he was encouraging, and actually invited me to stay on to clerk with him a second year. He also encouraged me to try to figure out what it was I wanted to do long term. He actually invited another woman to talk with me. She had clerked for one of the other judges and had gone on to work in D.C. public services. She talked about that work, and I thought, wow, these people were doing so much to help other people. I ended up applying there, and fortunately was blessed to get a job there. That was just awesome.

I learned something from that experience; that there were a lot of people who looked like me, who had similar life experiences, but they took a wrong turn. They did not have someone there like I did to tell them that education and working hard are so important. They did not get the advice I got from my home economics teacher and the lawyers, so they went down a different path. Their role models in the community were drug dealers and people who were stealing from stores. They ended up going in the opposite direction.

I enjoyed that work, and I enjoyed representing people who needed someone in their corner. I was a trial attorney for eight years, and then became the deputy director of the agency for three or four years. While I was working as deputy director, the court underwent a sort of revitalization of their family court division and they created the family court. They also created a magistrate judge position. Before that change, the associate judges handled the various matters, like family court matters, criminal matters and civil matters, they handled everything. But the magistrate judge was to be a dedicated judge for family court, to handle those cases and really give the time and attention those cases deserved. So, when I learned of the new magistrate judge position, I talked with the director and told her I was planning to apply for it. She initially responded that I did not have the experience for it because I had only worked criminal cases, not family cases, and one of the requirements of the position was to be experienced with family cases. I then told her that I grew up in foster care and so I knew a little something about what that life is like, and maybe that could be of value to the kids. She immediately responded that I should apply for it, that my experience going through the system may be enough, that I should try for it.

When I went to the interview I think there were ten to twelve judges on the interview panel. They said they knew my reputation from trying criminal cases, but what did I know about family law? I said, well, aside from handling juvenile delinquency cases for about a year, I grew up in foster care. My experiences in foster care then became part of the conversation. I mean, in other interviews they are interested in your skill set and your temperament, but they were very interested in what going through foster care was like and how I managed to get into law school. How had I managed not to become one of those statistics? I ended up getting the job.

One big worry I had initially when I became a magistrate judge was how I would relate to the parents. I knew I could relate to the kids, that I could be a real ear for them, someone who truly understood their position, their plight, what they were feeling and going through. But, I worried that I would not understand the parents well enough, because I still had a lot of bitterness and anger toward my mother. I wondered how I would treat these parents who did not love their children, because I felt that my mother did not love me enough to make a home for us.

Fortunately, though, once I heard their stories, I saw there was more to these people than the substance addiction, the physical abuse and neglect that brought them to the attention of the agency. There was much more to these folks. They had their own life stories that had not been that good. Some of them grew up in foster care, some of them had teenage parents who did not know how to parent and, you know, you learn from what you see. They learned from the behavior of the adults in their lives. As long as you are seeing other people who are drinking, drugging, being abusive, or being inattentive, that is what you become if you do not see another side. If you do not see people who get an education, who work every day, who strive to be their best, then what difference do you know?

So, I was able to talk to the parents. I let them know that when their kids are in their care, the kids are scared, and they do not know what is going on. I told them they really needed to work hard to get their kids back and that if they were not willing to work hard then make a decision early on that you are not going to interfere with their chance for permanency with someone else. I found that I could be fair to the parents. I learned that whatever it was that brought the kids into foster care was not the sum total of who these parents were. They were more than that and they needed to have a chance, an opportunity to get their lives together and to get their children back. It was a great job, and I did that for fourteen years.

During those years, I would sit there and see the kids that came through the court, and just did not see a lot of permanency. So, year after year of seeing some of the same kids over and over, I wanted to take every child home so they could have a stable life. Eventually my husband and I decided it might be nice to adopt one child. At that point, we had an adult son, so adopting one older child was initially our goal, someone between the ages of maybe ten and fourteen. We wanted a child who had maybe bounced around from home to home and needed something stable. That age range is sometimes a hard age range to place into adoption because they have had so many experiences and they are angry. People do not want to put up with some of the behaviors that come with the kids in that age range. They may strike out at the very people who are trying to help them, and this can be difficult for some people to understand.

But once we finished the process; became eligible to adopt,

got licensed and everything, the social worker had a different idea. She thought we should adopt two very small children. I had actually been looking at a couple of older kids for adoption, but they did not want to be adopted. They had not really lived together even though they were biological siblings. They were in with foster families and did not want to be adopted. So, my husband and I considered adopting the two little ones the social worker had recommended. We talked with our adult son about whether he would be willing to raise them if for some reason my husband and I were unable to raise them to adulthood. Would he take them and raise them? He said yes. You know, without him agreeing to this we would not have adopted the two little ones. Tragically, about a year after the adoption, my husband passed. I moved down to North Carolina where my son is and he is helping me raise them.

That is basically my story. I am still insecure sometimes and I still have times where I am down. I still question a whole bunch of things, but, you know, my two little ones are helping me to not wear that on my sleeve so much. I do not want them to have these same insecurities. I try not to let them hear me say I cannot do something or hear some of the other things that can come out of my mouth because I am still insecure about some things, about what I can and cannot do. I try to really encourage them.

Dominique

Washington, D.C.

Out of all the things I've been labeled, called, or identified as, the term foster child hurt me the most. It was not only what other kids used to call me to humiliate me, it carried an ugly stigma of pity as if I was always someone else's responsibility. Ultimately, the message I received from it all was that I was a mistake, or that I was unwanted.

I entered the foster care system in California at just one day old when I tested positive for drugs. Due to the negligence of both the hospital and the foster care system, my birth went undocumented for eighteen years. I was a foster child without access to any identity. This caused a delay in my life. I could not apply for college because I could not access financial aid. I could not get an ID, take drivers education, or apply for government assistance. I could not legally support myself.

My story is rare in how dramatic my transition out of care was. But it is not uncommon for youth to be so unprepared when they leave foster care. At age twenty-six, more than a third have experienced homelessness. Only six percent have completed a two or four-year college. Almost half are not working. Nearly sixty percent of men and thirty percent of women have been convicted of a crime.

My story wouldn't be complete without mentioning the women who changed my life. My "mother" began hosting me when I was nine. She provided me with normalcy, with things like birthday parties, Saturdays at amusement parks, family dinners, and self-confidence. Also, my mentor, who not only recommended me for a college scholarship, she supported me through the process of applying to my dream school. She drove two hours to pick me up from my college dorm to drive me to every court date so I could get a birth certificate and social security number.

I am thankful to share my story, to educate those who want to learn about the foster care system and to let others who are in care know that you are powerful. No matter where you are or what has happened, or how hard it seems, you will get the happiness you deserve.

Tessa

Florida

I didn't always work with kids in foster care. I spent ten years working with medical software and was on a medical campus doing large scale promotional and fundraising campaigns, and community relations. One reason I was at the university for so long was because I was supporting people who were researching a cure for cancer. Both of my parents are cancer survivors, so I felt I was almost saving myself by making sure these people were successful.

It really meant something to me to have a job that was also part of a mission. I was really fortunate to get my MBA on a scholarship, but unfortunate when they got a new dean and there were a bunch of layoffs. A whole line of us, including my boss, were laid off. When I left there I went to work with a software company. I built out their training website. That company ended up being bought out by another company. I was offered a position with the new company, but I didn't want to do it. That kind of analytical work was very easy for me, but it was not very rewarding.

At the time, I was comfortable enough financially that I could take some time off, so I did. I just needed a break to think about what my next steps in life would be. I had been raised by an Episcopalian minister, and my father had some flaws. Because of my dad's flaws, early on I had decided that the church was flawed. I hadn't been to church in about fifteen years, and I was feeling a little lost in life.

I decided to take some time away and go to Spain to hike the Camino de Santiago trail. This route had been the sacred pilgrimage of St. James the Great, one of the apostles of Jesus. At the end of that hike, I ended up on my knees in a cathedral in Santiago where St. James was buried. You know, when you read about the Camino trail you hear that it breaks you physically, but that it also breaks you spiritually and then it puts you back together. There were problems I went onto the Camino with, thinking they would be fixed. But I still had them when I got to the end at the cathedral in Santiago.

There I was at the cathedral on my knees, and I prayed, God do you want me to go back to school, go back to seminary and become a minister? God said, no, and I said okay. Do you want me to give up everything and become like a Mother Theresa? When I prayed this, I remember thinking about my washer and dryer, because I had a really nice, high-end washer and dryer set and I really didn't want to give those up. But I was willing to do whatever God told me to do. God said, no. So, I returned home with this thought of, what am I going to do in my life to bring back meaning to my work?

I applied for one job and was hired as a total outsider with no experience. I was brought in to run a family center. It was a very small family center and thank God nothing bad happened while I was there because I had no experience going into it. I have always taken work really seriously, so I studied the budget, I studied the programs, and after a couple of months there I was running a summer camp. I had no experience running this type of thing.

I had a person at the time who reported to me and she had a little experience with running a camp. She sent me incident reports in the mornings and they always had the same names on them. We had an agreement to allow five kids to attend the camp for free from a local non-profit dedicated to helping and housing formerly abused and neglected kids that had been removed from their homes. There was this one kid from that organization, I will call him Michael but that's not his real name, and every morning he was biting the kid next to him. He was about five or six years old. So, I kept looking at those reports and thinking there was something more there.

Each morning as the kids arrived and checked in, they would sit down with the counselors for breakfast, and then they got some crayons to color for about thirty minutes or so while kids were checking in. One morning I sat down with the kids for breakfast so I could see how Michael interacted with the others. One of the other kids reached over Michael to grab a crayon, because every other kid at the table knew how to use the crayons. They had used crayons before and they had shared before. They knew that if they put a crayon back, they would get to use it again after someone else was finished. But, when someone reached over to take one near Michael he tried to bite them. He had never shared crayons before, and never had his own. He thought he would not get to use them again if someone else took them. So, when that happened I talked with him about it, and we talked about sharing. Knowing that he came from the children's home and that there was probably a really bad story of abuse or abandonment, I just took a very loving but firm approach with him when I talked about these things.

There were also opportunities at camp to talk about sportsmanship with Michael and the other kids, and, you know, why you don't throw the football at a girl. You might like her, but there are other ways to show her. You can go sit next to her, or maybe when you go to the snack table you bring her back a juice. Michael and the other kids just touched me deeply that summer. When camp came to an end we had a party and gave out awards. A couple of us went to visit Michael at the children's home, and we gave him a basketball and a football. We wrote his name with a permanent marker on both balls, so he would have his own.

A couple of months went by and my boss came in and said we had just received a grant, six thousand dollars for the organization, but we needed to deliver free swimming lessons to one hundred kids under the age of ten within the next couple of weeks. So, as we were scrambling to find enough kids, I thought of the children's home and called over there to their activities coordinator. They transport their kids to activities, so I knew we could get enough kids quickly for the lessons. We would just work around their schedule. They show up, and we put them in swimming classes.

It worked. They brought over many kids and they were getting into the pool and blowing bubbles. But then I noticed my buddy, Michael, right by the side of the pool, not getting in. He had on a long-sleeved cotton shirt, but cotton wasn't allowed in the pool because it clogged the filters. What I had not focused on during summer camp was that he went through the whole summer with long-sleeved shirts on. It never occurred to me why, it never registered. I went over and talked to him. He told me that he didn't want to show his arms. He said, "I can't show my arms." We found one of the lifeguard shirts made of a different material, so Michael went into the bathroom and switched out his shirts, and we got him into the water blowing bubbles. Within a couple of days he was retrieving stuff from the bottom of the pool, and a couple days after that he was in the deep end swimming around and high fiving the teacher like a natural and gifted athlete. Later, I talked to his chaperones, the staff from the children's home, and learned the reason he didn't want to show his arms was because his mother had burned him. His entire arm was covered in cigarette and cigar burns. I still struggle with the thought of this.

That is something I have always really struggled with, hearing about children being abused. As a child, I had first-hand experience with abuse and abandonment. I really feel for these children because I know how much work and how long it took me to get over those things. So his chaperones were really amazing. The staff at the children's home was really amazing, because these were people who worked twenty-four hours a day, seven days a week all year long with these children.

Michael just really touched me in a very profound way that summer. That camp was more than just fun for me; it was about giving a child structure and talking to a child about the right thing to do versus the wrong thing. I also learned about other kids from the children's home, and some of the stories will haunt me for the rest of my life. The staff told me there was a girl in their program that had been kept outside in a dog kennel, with dogs. She walked on all fours, she ate out of a bowl on the floor, and she barked. When I heard that I really stepped back and started to think about these children. I really struggled with understanding how things like this could be done to children.

That fall, I decided to apply for a position at the children's home. I wanted to do something meaningful with my life and help these children who had been so hurt. I reached out to my network and that was when I found out about a fundraising position there. I was really blessed, and got the job. I feel like it is such an amazing blessing to be a part of their mission. I'm a really strong person but let me tell you I cry about once a week at work. During those times, I think back to my time at the cathedral in Spain and I think about what God really wants me to do with my life. The answer I always get back is that I should be of service to these children. I'm just so grateful that I made the decision to get His mission back into what I do.

Charell

New York

I was born in Philadelphia, but I am from New York. I spent a lot of time in and out of foster care and was reunified with my family when I was about ten or eleven. I spent a couple of years living with family, and then I got a scholarship to go to boarding school in Arizona. It was a working cattle ranch boarding school, so I learned to horseback ride, rock climb and camp. I spent four years out there, then went to Boston for college. I spent three and a half years there, and then spent a semester abroad in London. I travelled to Spain and France, and just loved Paris. I went to

Morocco and finished my last semester there. Then I came back, graduated, and then started working.

I did various public relations jobs in different agencies for about thirteen years, and then a couple years ago I decided I wanted to move to the journalism side. I freelance now. I'm a blogger, and a journalist. I also do some event planning and public relations work. I have loved writing for a really long time and my blog has been doing pretty well. I write about fashion, beauty, technology, and culture on my site. I also contribute to some other sites and have my own column on those sites, including a tech site. I also do some on-camera work and contribute to a local news show every once in a while. It's been working out very well.

It was an interesting journey for me, growing up in foster care. I did a lot of time in foster care, including kinship care with relatives. Overall, it was a rough time and going through foster care was very traumatic. Even though I was reunified with my family at one point, it was still difficult. We butted heads a lot when I was a kid and I lived with them for only a very short time. I am glad I made the decision to go to boarding school, but, yeah, I'm still dealing with the effects of my early life.

I got married about two years ago. It still feels like the newlywed stage. It's interesting, there are still moments from foster care that bubble up to the surface and things that still affect me. I think for others who did not go through the system, through foster care, these things don't happen in the same way. You have these moments of, I don't want to say depression, but just frustration. You know, you will always have these sudden moments of frustration.

My husband has learned to deal with it and help me cope, but I have always been a crier. So my way of coping with a lot of stress is to just break down and cry. I cry for a few minutes. Then I just feel relieved and I'm able to move forward from that point. This can be very jarring to people because they don't want to see you crying, they think something is terribly wrong. No, this is just how I deal with stress, and how I dealt with stress when I was younger and in foster care.

Usually, when you cry people leave you alone, and that may be the only alone time you get in foster care. If you are in a crowded apartment with a lot of kids, or if someone is yelling at you and you are in a violent situation, sometimes crying is a good way to diffuse the situation. It becomes a security blanket, a safety mechanism, and so it has always been how I deal with pressure and stress. I have been trying to learn how to manage it a little more, you know, if I feel it coming on I will walk away, that sort of thing. But I feel like I'm in a good space in my career now, where I just tell people, you know, I may start crying, don't worry about it. I will be okay. It takes a long time to get to that point though, where you feel comfortable being honest about who you are.

I started volunteering recently on two foster care boards, charities here in New York. One is a Court Appointed Special Advocate organization. They do amazing work and I am honored to be on their board. I am helping them plan an event that is happening soon, a luncheon to raise some money. I also just joined the board of another, newer organization for foster youth who aged out of foster care. They specifically focus on trying to find solutions for youth living on their own for the first time. When you age out at twenty-one, the city kind of says good luck, and then they leave you. It's not just that the youth don't have enough money to pay rent, they have not learned some of the basics to help them survive. People don't think youth will need help with little things like furnishing an apartment and buying groceries, because people with families and other support have been taught about these things. But these youth really didn't have that support. So that organization is really trying to bridge that gap and help them with those things.

I get to spend a lot of time with foster youth now, especially now that I am volunteering with these two charities. I actually spent some time with a youth a couple weeks ago at a networking event that happens every Wednesday. One of the youth in our program, she is a young adult who just graduated from college and is heading to law school. This is a huge accomplishment, but she was feeling frustrated because she could not find a job in the legal field. So, the founder of the organization mentioned she should come to the networking group, that several lawyers would be there, and she could at least make some connections. She came, and it was just really wonderful to hear her talk about herself, and it was wonderful to see how those lawyers gravitated toward helping her. I felt really proud to see that happen and to help make connections with her. I love being in a position where I can help other foster youth. I want everyone to know that sometimes it is just that little bit of support that makes all the difference.

I think that is what a lot of foster youth really need, people willing to just open the door. It is really hard to go through the foster care system. I mean, you know the statistics. What is it, less than ten percent of foster youth actually graduate college? It is something crazy like that. One in five will be homeless in their lifetime. It is the little things that people can do that really make a difference. Opening their hearts up a little bit can go a long way toward helping someone who wants to do better; who wants to succeed.

I wish more youth in foster care got to travel. I love to travel. Paris is my favorite city in the world. I have been to France about five times now. I have been to Morocco and Spain. I have been to almost every major city in the United States. I have been fortunate to see a lot of the country and have been able to chat with a lot of people in different areas. Just being out of your normal environment and being exposed to something different is huge. It is one of the reasons I'm really glad I went to boarding school. It was a big culture shock for me to move from Harlem to a working cattle ranch in Arizona. I went from being, you know, in the majority here in this world, to a place where I was one of ten black students, and all the black students were there on scholarships. They were all scholarship kids, so it was just a very different environment to go to school with, you know, wealthy youth. But, it was also good in that it was the first time I got to see what two parent households look like, and what can be accomplished when you have that sort of support.

In boarding school, they had nights when there were sit-down dinners. That was really the first time I had a sit-down dinner. Even on holidays, my family did not do sit down dinners, and none of the foster families I lived with had sit down dinners. So that was a jarring experience, to have to sit down and talk about what we did that day. It was very, very different and I am thankful for that experience. I am thankful for the friends I still have from boarding school.

When I arrived at boarding school it was very difficult to adjust, but when I finished I was looking at my life, my world in New York, through a very different lens. You know, growing up there is no place bigger than New York City, even if you are only in a ten-block radius, because that was the distance I was allowed to travel by myself when I was young. I could ride my bike within ten blocks of my house without being in trouble. But when I left New York, I realized how much bigger the world is, and I got to see there are other places that are just spectacular. There is so much out there. New York is wonderful, and I love New York. New York is my first love. But it is great to see what else is out there and to realize just how big the world really is with all its different cultures.

I wish more foster youth had the opportunity to get out of their immediate situations, if only for a day, to get a different perspective on how the rest of the world operates. This would be helpful especially if they are in a bad home, or a bad situation, because everything can feel so defeating. It can feel like everything is against you. It can be good to just get away and see that there is so much more going on, that there is so much more to look forward to. It can change how you deal with the situation you are in. I am really thankful that I was able to travel and see other parts of the country outside of New York and my immediate situation.

Growing up in foster care shaped my views on raising a family, and what that means to me and my husband. For the longest time I would say that I did not want to have any children; that I wanted to adopt and foster instead. It wasn't until I met my husband that I realized this view was more out of fear on my part, fear of perpetuating the things that had happened in my family and to me. That was eye-opening for me, and we are actually planning our family now. It is very exciting, and we want to have one, and then foster and adopt one as well. The thought of this is really exciting, but it took me being with someone I was really comfortable with and exploring what my fears really were for me to get there. When I look at my history of how I ended up in care and why that was, I look at what happened to my mom, and, you know, her siblings and then my grandmother. They all experienced so much trauma, and I was afraid of perpetuating that, afraid of passing that on.

The whole conversation of nature versus nurture, it's scary, terrifying. So, yeah, I always thought that I would not have kids. I was just going to foster and adopt. There are so many kids out there who need love and a loving family. I still believe that, but the conversations with my husband made me realize what I was afraid of. I'm so glad to have him, to have been able to work that out in my head and realize it is not something to be feared.

I think I can offer a kid I adopt or a kid we have more than what I had when I was young. I can offer more love and support than I had, so I don't think things will turn out the way they did in the history of my family. That is refreshing to feel that way, it is a relief. It is those sorts of conversations that you don't get unless you have another support person in your life. You don't get to work that out unless you have someone who is willing to listen and help you get to the heart of the issue. My husband is very good at that.

Lately, I have just been doing a lot of writing and pitching stories to editors. My whole life is centered around my site now, my blog, and doing stories on fashion, beauty and technology. I spend a lot of time trying to come up with new story ideas and then if it won't be for my site, it is about pitching to my editors or producers for stories they can use in their outlets as well. That has been going really well lately, which is really good. My blog is seeing an uptick in traffic, so I'm very proud of that. I won't say it is like having a baby, because it's not, but it has been pretty difficult to start and sort of keep that going, so I'm proud of it. There are those days when you write a story and you post it, share it and promote it, and then no one is reading it. I think, why would no one read it, it's such a good story? But, then there are stories that I am surprised become so popular. Sometimes I do the research and I do all the interviews, but I'm just not where my audience is thinking that day. I'm not where their heads are.

I also love camera work. I did a couple of pilots for a show. They haven't been picked up, but, knock on wood, hopefully one of them will get picked up. I have been pitching everything myself, but you know everyone else has agents and managers. This is a whole new world for me. I am on my third pilot right now, it is like a batting average. The more you do, you just hope one lands to sort of take it to the next step. I liked all three of the concepts I did, and they are all with different producers. We'll see if any of them come through. I'm very excited about it.

As I get older, I am moving more into leveraging my history, my experiences, to bring awareness for foster youth. I think it is really important to tell your story, to be a visual representation, because people have such misconstrued ideas of what foster kids look like and what being in foster care means. I try, as much as possible, to give them a positive view. I don't rewrite what my experience was, but I want people to see what a person who has gone through foster care actually looks like. I want people to see what a person who goes through that experience is capable of.

When I graduated and got my first couple of jobs, I did not want to tell people I had been in foster care. There were a few times I let it slip, and people would look at me differently. I could see it in their faces; they were judging me because they had all these misconstrued ideas about foster care. People would say to me that foster kids were in care because they had done something wrong, like juvenile detention. That is absolutely one hundred percent incorrect. Youth are in foster care because something terrible happened in the family and their parents could not take care of them properly. The kids themselves have done nothing wrong. These misconceptions harm them if they are in a job interview and they let it slip. There is a view that there is a criminal sitting across the table and that is not fair. So I try to be a positive representation of what is possible for foster youth.

Kids in foster care are just normal kids. They have problems just like everyone else. Just because a youth is in foster care means nothing about what they can or cannot accomplish. If anything, the youth I know who went through foster care tend to be harder workers. They tend to have a greater understanding, especially in the city, of how to get things done. They do not want to fail. There is a lot of pressure.

This is something I still struggle with, that fear of failing. I worry about being judged if I fail, thinking that the world will be over if I have a moment of failure. That is something we former foster youth struggle with, but there is nothing about foster youth that means they are less than others, or that they cannot get something done. There are so many strikes against them just because they went through foster care. I want to do more opportunities like this book, more of sharing my story, because I want to make sure people know what the lives of kids that go through foster care can look like. They are deserving of a normal life, especially after they come out on the other side of everything they had to deal with. There should be no reason why anyone should try to keep that from them. Look at them the same as everyone else.

If I have something to say to kids in foster care it is this: you are not crazy. When you are in foster care, it is very easy to feel like you are the crazy one. You live in this tumultuous environment and adults are not doing what they are supposed to do. You are in this situation where your gut is always telling you this is wrong. So, I want to let foster kids know you are not crazy. You are in an unfair situation. I'm sorry that you're in this situation, but you should know that it won't always be this way. There will come a point when you will get to choose what you want for yourself, when you get to choose where you go in life. You need to hold that fact very close to you. You get to be excited about that day, and you should prepare for it. You should prepare for what that day looks like, and don't be afraid to ask for more. Don't be afraid to ask about, college, about boarding schools. Don't be afraid to ask questions. If the foster parent or the home you are in is not giving you information on what happens next, don't be afraid to ask those questions. If you are about to age out; ask questions. What happens once I age out? What opportunities or what resources are available to me? Ask those questions and don't let them dismiss you. You need to be willing to push yourself through, especially when other people are not going to. I wish I could say it will be easy, but it won't be. But you get to want more for yourself.

For anyone wanting to help foster youth, I say it is the little things that matter. If you are able to spend some time with a youth, it is those little moments that are amazing. Even if you are only able to spend an afternoon and not actually adopt or become a foster parent, please do it. Also, if you ever come across a youth and they tell you they were or are in foster care, fix your face. Don't give that look of, oh, you must be terrible. Give them a word of encouragement. Say something like, that must have been really hard. I'm so proud of you for making it through. It's those small moments of encouragement that can make a world of difference. Growing up in care you get so little of that. You get so little of those moments of encouragement.

People have these fairytale ideas of what foster care is, or they have these terrible ideas of what foster care is and what foster youth are like. I suggest everyone should be open to hearing what it is actually like. Do your homework and realize that foster kids are just normal kids. They are not bad kids, they have done nothing wrong and yet everything has been taken from them. I mean, imagine what your life would have been like if when you were four or five years old everything you knew was just suddenly taken away. Good or bad, it was just no longer there. How would you want someone to treat you? If you can think in that way and be willing to have an open perspective, an open mind, you can try to find some common ground. Just be a decent human being to these kids. I think that would go a long way.

I would love for there to be more foster parents in the system, good foster parents in the system. That is needed, definitely first and foremost, but until we get to that point we can all be just a little more understanding and maybe give some of our time. Kids in foster care are just normal kids, except they don't have anyone in their corner. We can be there for them, and even small things we do can make a big impact.

Brittany

Illinois

I started off with no children thinking I was infertile and went to six children including one biological daughter. The minute I started doing foster care and adopting kids, I found out I was pregnant. Yeah, kind of crazy.

I learned about the foster care system through a friend. At the time, I never thought I would be able to have of a child on my own, and I wanted children in my home. I had a four-bedroom house and no children except my stepdaughter who is with us every now and then. So I looked into it, did some research, and went with a private agency. It started from there. I ended up fostering three, four, five, then six kids before my adopted son came into my home.

He was in foster care his whole life, since he was born. When

I got him he was just turning seven. He's now ten. We adopted him when he was nine years old. He was literally in foster care for nine years, going from home, to home, to home. He began with his biological family, then ended up in traditional foster care, and then has been in my home ever since. After we adopted him, I fostered four more children and they all returned home, thankfully.

While I was fostering, I uploaded our family profile on adoptuskids.org, because I wanted to adopt more children. A caseworker then reached out to me for a sibling group of six. We could not take six kids at that time, so we took the two oldest children who are now sixteen and fifteen. We are just around the corner with their adoptions. After that, I now have a seventeen-year-old that came into our home about six month ago, and we are in the process of adopting her too.

When we started foster care, I was working as a paralegal. Then I left that job to join a non-profit Lutheran organization that provides social services for children in foster care, because as you may be aware, Illinois is dead last in finding permanency for children in foster care. We have the most children in residential facilities, hospitals, you name it. So the Director of Human Services at the time wanted to give every agency in Illinois the opportunity to come up with a plan to get kids out of residential homes and into traditional foster home placements. A lot of our kids in residential care are there due to severe behavioral and emotional issues which could be due to hospitalization or other things. A ton of agencies submitted proposals and the Director choose three agencies, one of them being ours, and we have a model now that we have adopted.

The model is pretty much about rewarding for good behavior. This is not a normal model for children in foster care, but normal to us. I know kids in foster care, certain good behaviors are just not normal from them. So we reward them for that, and it is an incentive-based program. There's a ton of support, too, for the foster parents. It's like no other program you've seen. It's an amazing program.

Once the foster parents I recruit for the program have a child placed in their home they receive a call from me every day, Monday through Friday, just to check on them and the behaviors of the children from the day before. There is also a mandatory weekly support group meeting, and we are on-call twenty-four seven for them. We go to the houses if we need to.

We placed a few children several months ago, so it's early in the program and still fairly new. One of our children is an eight-year-old. Before starting this program she had been in the hospital three times in a four-month period for suicidal ideation, running away from home, going into traffic, and trying to jump out of moving vehicles to harm herself. She would run away probably two or three times a week. Since we started this program, we are going on two months without her running away. So, the results are wonderful.

So that's what I do now. I recruit foster parents for this program. It's a tough job. It's hard to recruit foster parents for children who are in residential facilities, so hopefully this program is successful. We do have a five-year grant. If it is successful, the goal is to implement this program into the state agency for more foster families to use. People have asked me why I stopped being a paralegal, because I made really good money. I left that job to go into social work, where you don't make money. It is because I believe that this program will help hundreds of kids. They deserve it; the older children especially deserve a loving home. They deserve the stability.

I believe it will be a successful program. It has already proven to be successful, and I want nothing more. In my experience, unfortunately, people say no to teens because they have their own special issues that are hard to deal with. But I truly, truly believe that teenagers are wonderful. People who say no, they don't know what they are missing. And I truly believe that if I can recruit really good foster parents, we can get children out of residential facilities and into good loving foster homes. Eventually they could even return home to either mom or dad, or be adopted out. Before we can even take them into our program we have to have an after-care family for them, whether that is mom, dad, another biological family member or an adoptive parent. It's a lot of work, but we are required to have an aftercare family for them. So that's the goal, and it's my goal to get every kid out of residential facilities. I know it's not going to happen for all of them, but I want to get as many kids as possible out of residential facilities and into foster homes.

For my own family, we are very much a blended family. My husband and I are Caucasian. We have two Caucasian daughters, and an African American son, he's ten. We also have an African American daughter, and she also identifies as a male. Then we have two older boys who are Mexican. So, we are a very blended family, and I love that. It's unique. We learn a lot from one another. Every day is a new day to learn something new about each other's cultures, the way we were raised, and how we could mix all of our traditions together. Even more during the holidays, it's crazy, but my family is complete. My three older ones are adopted, and I had to hand in my foster license only because I don't have any more room.

I have my older children and one of them, especially, experienced some pretty significant trauma in early life. Very, very significant. It was challenging to work around. There were times, unfortunately, when I contemplated giving notice to return the child because of some of the behaviors. Well, in the past anyway. But at the end of the day, my husband and I decided that this is our child. I love this child more than I have ever loved anybody else, same with all of my children. I love my children equally, my biological children and my adoptive children. I love them all the same and I kept thinking, what if this child was my biological child? Who, as a parent, can say, I'm giving a notice to return my child? I couldn't bring my heart to do that. My heart aches for this child so much, and this child is just so much better now.

For foster kids out there, I want you to know there is a home out there that will love you and treat you with respect and kindness. For anyone who potentially would want to be a foster parent, I say do it. There are definitely challenges and tons of hurdles, but at the end of the day, knowing my kids have a safe home and loving parents is well worth it. For foster families, I wish, and I pray and I hope that you will consider every age, zero to eighteen, because these children need a home. Even the older ones, they are just children. I am so in love with my children. It was the best decision I ever made in my life.

$\mathcal{S}arah$

Washington, D.C.

In my transition into foster care, I had six placements in six months. I really wanted to stay in the same school so I could graduate from there, so I asked a friend if I could stay with her. She had been in foster care and was adopted at that point, but they didn't have room. She had an aunt, though, who could take me in. So, I ended up living with her aunt and I still keep in touch with her to this day. I call her Aunt Linda.

It was a struggle at first because it was a very different culture, living with her versus living with my family. I went from living in a trailer in the suburbs with a family member who is white and Catholic to living in the city with a strong-willed African American woman who was very Christian. She said that if I was going to live in her house I had to go to church. She asked if I was Christian. I told her yes, that I was Catholic. So I went to church with her and everyone was jumping around and speaking in tongues. I was sitting there shocked. She noticed and said, "I take it you are not Christian?" I asked, "Isn't Catholic, Christian?" She said, "Yes, but it's different. We may have to find a church you are more comfortable with."

We just laughed about that. She was really good. She made her house my home. One of the first things she said to me was that if there is something in the house I wanted, I could have it. If it was not in the house, I could add it to the weekly shopping list. If I wanted cookies, I could have them. Just to test the limits, I made a list that was made up of junk foods and she bought it all. I couldn't believe it. She did have some rules. She made dinners, she made me do chores and she wouldn't let me out of the house in pajamas. She told me to dress like I was going to school. It was the structure I wanted, that I didn't have before. I was with her for about five years, from the age of sixteen to twenty-one.

I went to community college. Most people went to community college for three to four years, and I graduated in two. I wanted to be done and move on. I then transferred to a four-year college and studied international relations, Spanish and Latin American studies. I studied in Spain during the summer of my first year. I went there knowing very little Spanish and I remember getting on the plane being so nervous and then we landed, everything was in Spanish. I thought to myself, what did I do? I was young and in foster care, and here I was all of a sudden in Spain, not knowing the language at all, it was just crazy. It didn't really sink in until day two or three, and I just cried and cried. After I cried for a while I realized it was an opportunity that no one in my family ever had, and that I should really appreciate it. I told myself you can do it, you are already here and you are not going to pay extra to go back home early. I made it work.

Luckily, I had a really cool roommate in Spain. She was such a free-spirit. We went out and made friends with some of the Spanish locals. They took us to all the best places and we hung out with their family. I ended up learning more Spanish than many of the other people there because I went out of my comfort zone. I still keep in contact with those people, and it's been almost eleven years. I feel like those connections will last a lifetime.

Spain was so magical. They had live music in the square, everyone was out at night and the weather was beautiful all the time. That trip sparked my interest in learning Spanish and salsa dancing, and it pushed me to come out of my comfort zone. When I was in high school, I never pushed myself. After going to Spain, I wanted to take more Spanish classes, not because they were required, but because I liked it. By the time I was about to graduate from college I was taking only Spanish classes. So, it was awesome to see that progression.

I also had the opportunity during college to go to El Salvador twice for a couple of weeks. On my first trip I did not realize how dangerous it could be. I flew by myself to meet up with the group and I was on the last flight into the airport, so when I arrived no one was there. I didn't have a phone to call my group and I wasn't sure of the address, but I had the paper they gave me so I took a random taxi and got there. Everyone was crowded around the door of the hostel when I arrived and they said, "Sarah, what did you do? Do you not realize when it's late here it is dangerous?" I just said, "Well, I made it!" The crazy stuff you do when you're young, you just don't realize. Luckily, I was never in a really dangerous situation there; that was the closest I ever came to danger.

When I woke up that first morning in El Salvador we did a walking tour of our neighborhood and there were guys with huge guns guarding stores and different things. I thought to myself, maybe it actually is dangerous. Maybe I should have payed attention to their instructions. I hadn't read the fine print on the paperwork that said don't travel by yourself, and call when you land at the airport, don't take a random taxi. It was crazy, but I loved El Salvador. We participated in a human rights delegation.

I went with a program that brought college-aged kids down and they taught us about the effects of the war. We worked with kids, and we did workshops on how to keep kids away from gangs. Immigration was another focus when we were there.

Now I work with refugee settlements and unaccompanied minor programs; most of them are from Guatemala, Honduras, and El Salvador. I can't believe where I am right now. When I interviewed for my job I thought I blew it because I said the reason I was a good fit is because I had been in foster care. A couple of the people I lived with in foster care were actually part of those programs, one from El Salvador and one from Ecuador. I was very persistent when trying for this job, and I was comfortable saying that I had been in foster care. It makes me a stronger person.

The woman who interviewed me is a social worker and she just started crying during the interview. I thought, oh my goodness, I'm not going to get this job. Later on, when I was talking to her she said she just knew I was the one for the job. They had interviewed other people who were a little more qualified, but they said they knew I was the one because of my experience in foster care and my passion for the work. When I got the job, I thought, I am never leaving. Everyone in the office is so nice, and the vibe is so different from other jobs. You are there for the mission, you do your job and everyone gets along. They are kind to each other, and I feel like this is where I need to be.

Everyone in the office knows my background in foster care and I feel comfortable talking about it, which is great. I now have a great job, a wonderful daughter, good friends and ties to my biological family. I am not very close to my mom's side of the family, but at nineteen, I met my dad's parents. Ever since then we have been super close. We call each other at least twice a week, sometimes I call daily. Now, though, with this job and having a five-year-old, it can be hard to call often enough. If I wait too long to call, though, my grandma says she is coming from Delaware down to see me, to see what is going on and make sure I am okay. I love that.

Julia

Florida

I entered the foster care system in Miami, Florida when I was sixteen years old and a sophomore in high school. Before entering foster care we had been a small nuclear family of four, but had many internal challenges which seemed to catch up with us when we arrived in a new city. Upon entering foster care my life changed and the direction I was on shifted. I was on a new path.

I was placed in the West Miami suburbs with a single parent mother and teacher at the helm. She was different in many ways from me. She was culturally different, attended church, was the sole provider as both a mother and father, and she also had her own biological child and a recently adopted daughter. She was stable, handy around the house and led a structured routine. So when I arrived into her household I had to adjust to the rules, live with other people and even do chores, which was new to me. I quickly learned how to change a lightbulb, fix a flat tire on a bike, install flooring, pressure clean, mow the lawn and do the dishes, which later served as valuable skills when I aged out of foster care and lived on my own. She also taught me how to advocate for myself while in the system and encouraged me to seek assistance before I aged out of foster care. Luckily, a few months before aging out, I also met a wonderful local child welfare attorney who not only helped me to successfully emancipate and testify in court for the very first time, but would become my lawyer, employer, mentor and friend.

Aging out and gaining my own housing was a big milestone for me, and I was only able to do it because I had several supportive adult connections that made my transition easier. Through my assigned community-based care agency, I had found a trustworthy Independent Living supervisor who helped me receive assistance to furnish my new apartment with basic furniture. At first, I was reluctant to buy furniture because I had moved so often, however, he encouraged me to pick out a bed and a couch and together we moved me into my first apartment. I stayed there on my own for four years.

From there, I began going to college and at the same time working full time to financially support myself. While other youth had cars and parents to lean on, and other support systems, I had no car, no parents or other support and relied heavily on public transportation, even biking to night classes and several miles daily to and from work. During the holidays, I traveled to spend time with my family out of state so that I would not be alone. For six and a half years I worked as a youth organizer for a local, youth run, nonprofit organization that empowers current and former foster youth to become leaders and advocates within their communities. I had a steady income. I opened checking and savings accounts, and ultimately graduated with a bachelor's degree in social work after obtaining my associates degree.

Early on during my work we were able to identify a lot of issues within the foster care system in Miami that I myself, other teens, and adults had witnessed before privatization of the foster care system and that continued after privatization. So we began a grassroots campaign to make youths' voices heard, in order to influence change and systemic improvement. Because of my firsthand experience in the foster care system I became the expert in my own care and needs, and we quickly thought of something that had not been done before in our community. We created a group which empowered current and former foster youth to be heard in our child welfare community, not just seen and processed through the system. We wanted to use our voices and experiences to shape and improve the system.

Our effort began with a small but committed group of people around a table and evolved to become the first local foster youth advocacy group. Through this group, and with our sponsor, we developed a foster children's rights training manual, and provided trainings at large and well-known law firms in order to recruit pro-bono attorneys to represent a foster youth's voice and rights (versus having someone advocate for what the system thought was in a foster youth's best interests). We also held regular monthly meetings at a local community-based care agency where we informed youth of their rights, and connected them to local, legal resources. We also advocated for reforms in foster youth allowances, sibling placement and visitation, improvements to foster and adoptive homes, and more opportunities for normalcy for foster youth while in care. We asked for and received feedback from youth on what was occurring in their foster homes and how we could help to fix or improve things, whether for the individual, locally or even on a statewide level if it was necessary. Foster parents, case managers, adoptive parents and other adult supporters from the child welfare system attended our meetings, and on many nights, I would facilitate those meetings and trainings and I also facilitated our annual awards ceremonies for child welfare providers. We also hosted monthly holiday dinners for youth like me who needed somewhere to go for the holidays.

Our organization eventually linked up with a larger nonprofit organization in a neighboring county dedicated to advancing the rights of at-risk children, especially those in foster care, to expand the youth organization to other chapters and create a statewide foster youth advocacy group. The youth, along with adult supporters who created the organization, developed bylaws, elected officers, created a logo, set agenda items, and brought in guest speakers for trainings. We put into action all our voices and ideas. Miami became a leading chapter and worked with additional chapters established by founding youth members from Jacksonville, Orlando, Broward County, Brevard County and Lee County in Florida.

Throughout my years of involvement with the organization I worked hand-in-hand with our local chapter and on the statewide level, even serving as the organization's state vice-president for a term. In that organization, I was able to hone my skills with public speaking, training, and working with people at all levels. I read and learned about current legislation, proposed bill amendments, traveled to our state capitol in Tallahassee, and testified in front of the Florida House of Representatives and Senate, and to local representatives from my district and the greater Miami areas. As foster youth leaders in our organization, we also identified areas for proposed legislation to benefit all foster youth in Florida, such as keeping siblings together, the foster youth bill of rights, monitoring usage of psychotropic medications in foster homes and in lock down facilities, driver's licenses for foster youth and transporting foster youth's belongings in luggage versus trash bags. We also created a proposed normalcy bill, so that foster youth could be treated as regular teens just like their foster and adoptive parent's children were treated, versus being labeled as troubled youth. I, along with my peers, also managed to extend foster care in Florida to the age of twenty-one, and then to the age of twenty-three, to prevent foster youth homelessness upon aging out and provide more time to equip them with life skills so that they were better prepared to live on their own. I also helped to advocate for foster youth to receive a tuition waiver, so they could go to any public university or higher education institution for free.

Over the course of two summers, and with the help of my mentor, I applied to two national internships and was selected to serve as a congressional intern in Washington, D.C. through the Congressional Coalition on Adoption Institute and as a Foster Club All-Star from Florida, based out of Seaside Oregon. In both of those internships I lived in other states and traveled and shared living spaces with interns from other states who were around the same age and had also successfully aged out of foster care. On this macro level, I was able to see the larger foster care advocacy initiatives and reforms that were taking place on a national level. I also had a chance to discover how foster care operated in other states, and I learned about the experiences of foster youth in those states.

During those internships I had a larger platform to represent foster youth from across the United States, and use my own experiences and those of my peers in Florida to ask for action, seek change and further inspire others as a role model. While interning in Washington, D.C., I gave congressional tours of the House of Representatives to constituents from Florida, took notes at congressional hearings and even testified to congressmen and senators on several panels. While interning in Oregon, I and a fellow youth peer had the opportunity to draft literature to help youth age out of foster care. We provided trainings across the United States to large mixed audiences of over two hundred Court Appointed Special Advocates, Guardian Ad Litems, foster parents, adoptive parents and youth who were currently in foster care or had aged out of foster care, along with child case work providers and administrators. During my internships I met many great people and learned a lot about myself and was also able to pick up new skills to continue the work and mission I was fulfilling in Florida once I returned. Some of these skills I still use today in the community.

Around the time I was finishing college I married my college sweetheart and best friend who I had met when I was eighteen years old, just after I aged out of foster care. I met his family, we moved in together and I decided to see what other areas outside of foster care and my circle I could excel in. Although I wanted to put my degree to use, there was a lack of entry level professional jobs in social work around the time I graduated. I began to lose faith that I would find something rewarding and meaningful to do. Finally, after several months into the job search, an organization called me about a job, as they were starting a new youth prevention and empowerment initiative for at-risk youth living in Miami with co-occurring disorders, specifically mental illness and substance abuse. It was perfect for me, and I fit the position like a glove. Once again, I wore my leadership shoes to handle the foundational work of building a youth-led organization. During this time I worked with new community members, paraprofessionals and professionals in the mental health and substance abuse fields. This experience added to what I had done during my internships, and I gained more cultural and linguistic competence as I worked with diverse populations very different from myself. Eventually, I decided I wanted to push myself and diversify my work even more, so I applied for and began employment as a Child Advocate or case manager with the lead community-based foster care agency in Broward County Florida.

Looking back, I think it is funny how I ended up coming full circle, going from being in foster care, to aging out of foster care, to advocating on behalf of foster youth while I was in college and then on to serving the families and youth directly as a case manager in the reunification department of a foster care agency. While in foster care, I had no idea things would turn out this way. Today, I even work at the same middle school that I attended before I entered foster care, which blows my mind.

Being a case manager was not easy for me or others I worked with, but the work was rewarding, challenging and once again good training for me. Like all child advocates or case managers, I was held accountable for all aspects of a child's and family's care, and to every person involved in the case including the judges, the families and my own managers in my department. In this position, I learned what it was like to be under pressure, meet deadlines, carry a heavy workload and even be scrutinized at times, so I had to become more disciplined in my work, assertiveness, accountability and communications. I also fundamentally learned how caring for everyone as a professional is hard work that can break you down if you do not learn to take care of yourself. Self-care is another cardinal rule of social work. I left case management short of a year, and then returned to Miami.

Fast forward to today, I still live in Miami with my husband of eight years, and have won a Child Advocate award, have served in leadership positions for two consecutive years for another charitable organization, and have been in the field of social work and nonprofit organizations for thirteen years. In my current work I continue to wear many hats, from teen pregnancy prevention instructor to grant writing and fundraising for my nonprofit organization. I also help recruit new youth participants for our programs and establish relationships with different schools, staff and administrators. In my life today, I continue to have purpose, balance, stability and accomplishments. I also have dreams, and like most people, I want to have kids, a house and be successful, although I think I may already be successful. I do want more. I am on a journey of personal and professional growth, and on a path of never-ending learning. I am looking forward to what's to come and I am grateful for where I have been, because if I had not had those life experiences I would not be where I am now or discovered who I am, which is a humanitarian and an advocate.

Schylar

Washington, D.C.

I grew up in the Montana foster care system and now live and work in Washington, D.C., where I advocate at the national level on behalf of children in foster care. After I endured so much in the foster care system, I made it a lifelong goal to work to better the lives of foster kids. I started locally in Montana, volunteering with organizations that helped foster kids in different ways, but as I got older I wanted to do something more broadly in our country. Working in Washington was certainly not something I would have anticipated when I was a teenager in foster care in Montana, but my life has been more of a journey and fortunately things aligned at the right time to bring me to Washington.

My family moved from Oregon to Montana to look for work when I was six years old. I entered foster care that same year, and over the years I bounced through eleven different foster homes, two group homes, and two residential treatment facilities. At sixteen, I went into an independent living program and was in independent living until graduation day from high school, then that support was totally cut off because I was already eighteen. This was prior to legislation that was enacted in Montana that extended the age of foster care to twenty-one.

Although I am put together now, I aged out of foster care a mess and have overcome a lot. There was a whole, I would say, five to ten years of my life where there was a lot of trial and error, there were some successes and a lot of failures. After all of that, I have come to realize that every child needs a place to call home. For a long time I rejected having a family because I was so angry. You know, hate is a strong word, but I hated the word family, because there was nothing good about it to me. As I got older, though, I realized that I didn't really hate families, I hated that I had never had a family, and I hated that I had this deep need to be totally independent because of all that I had been through. What I didn't realize until I got older is that family not only keeps you from being alone, it provides the support you need to be truly independent, too. You can have both within a safe family.

Realizing this was something new to me and it took me many years to fully understand it. Even when I was twenty-five years old and adopted by my sixth-grade music teacher, I didn't quite grasp yet what it meant to have someone there for me, someone to support and love me no matter what. I got a dad through adoption, but our relationship had to evolve over the years and adoption was a little weird for us, because I was an adult and we had known each other for so many years because he had been my mentor since the sixth grade. We didn't know exactly what adoption meant for us and whether things would change, but we thought we would just do it and adapt as we went forward.

It has evolved over time, and most importantly I have someone there for my highs and lows, my happy moments and my embarrassing moments. I call him and just tell him everything, and that is something that has become important in my life. There is one person out there that all of this really, really matters to, and that is my adoptive dad. It took so long for me to truly understand what it meant to be adopted, because I had never had a family. Growing up in the foster care system made for challenges I will face the rest of my life, but I do now understand and cherish having a family.

As I mentioned, I was six when I moved to Montana, and we were living in a trailer in a small town in southwest Montana. That was when everything started to change. We were new to the community, so of course people were paying attention to us, and I was in school and teachers saw marks and things on me that were not normal. One time one of us had our hand burned as a punishment, by pushing it against an old space heater grill, so there was a grid on his hand. After that, I was removed from our home. Being removed is probably the most powerful aspect of my story and I remember the most detail about that day over everything else that happened over the years before and since.

I lived in some terrible foster homes, but even after all that happened in those homes, the original removal from my family home was the most powerful and terrible thing that happened, something I don't think I will ever forget. I was just old enough to have it burned into my memory. I was just getting in bed for the night, and I recall I had on footy pajamas, you know, those pajamas with the feet in them. We were living in a trailer that would be more like a camper trailer to most people. There was one bed in a tiny, tiny bedroom, and then the kitchen table turned into a tiny bed I would share.

We already had a social worker at the time, but we didn't know what was going on when a lady appeared at the door and then there were some noises at the door. The lady then came inside, looked at us and told us to come with her outside. Once we got outside, we saw a lot of police. I remember walking outside in front of our neighbors, and it seemed like the whole neighborhood came out to see what was going on when they saw the police cars arrive.

The police walked me across the gravel in my footy pajamas and put me in the back of a vehicle. I can still feel the gravel on my feet when I remember it. They ended up taking me to the social worker's office. This was late at night, I don't know, like nine at night, and they began to ask questions about what happened to me. They asked why I thought I got pulled from our home. I am sure it had to do with the marks on me and what people reported, but I did not find out until years later who called them.

I originally thought it must have been our neighbor who reported the abuse because we played with his daughter a lot and she was a close friend, but it ended up being a teacher I had at the time who made the call. I learned about the teacher years later at a foster care conference when I was a speaker for the event. This former teacher of mine came up to me and said that I might not remember her, but that I needed to know that she was the one. I didn't know what she was talking about at first, and then suddenly it hit me like a brick that she had been the one to call the police because of the abuse. I think I had a true post-traumatic episode when I learned that, and it was instant. It is really weird how such a memory can have such a strong impact on you.

She said she hoped I wasn't mad at her, and, of course, I told her no. I did have the opportunity to explain my initial reaction to her at a later time, that I had been so caught off guard when she first told me and I became overwhelmed with those same feelings I had as a child when I had been removed from my family, and it was such a shock to feel that way so many years later. I also told her that I realized she did what she had to do, and that it is important that people take those steps, but I was also very up front with her and told her that my life became worse after I was removed from my family. It was much worse in the foster care system than it had been with my family.

After I was removed and put into foster care, I was put in a place for children who are severely emotionally disturbed, though I did not know I was emotionally disturbed at the time.

I had issues that I didn't understand. I was a severe sleep walker and would wake up outside of the house and not remember what happened. Because of the trauma I experienced, I wet the bed and had nightmares until well beyond what I should have, and I was also very aggressive. After that initial placement for emotionally disturbed children, the foster care system bounced me around to many different places.

I went to five or six elementary schools within a very short period, and I also went to several different middle schools. I think the hardest part for me was that up until age twelve I wanted to be reunited with my family, but that was not the focus of the system at that time. Back then, I was part of something called the generation that waits. There was an emphasis on protecting kids through removal from the abusive or neglectful situations, but no emphasis on trying to keep the biological family intact or finding other long-term solutions. They would remove children from their homes and put them in foster care without any goal toward reuniting them with their families, the ties were just severed in an instant. This perspective also meant there was no emphasis on finding adoptive families or trying for any sort of long-term family solution. The goal of the system was just to keep a roof over a kid's head at any given point.

For so many years, I wanted my family back and I tried to find ways to communicate with them but was never successful, this was before social media and cell phones. Then, after bouncing around from home to home for years, I met my sixth-grade music teacher and he ultimately became my adoptive father when I was twenty-five. What is interesting, though, is that he wanted to adopt me many years before that, probably before I lived in a third of the most severe foster homes, but he was a single man with no wife, so that caused a problem. The state denied him, and then told me I was unadoptable and what made things worse is that when they denied him from adopting me, my foster mom at the time severed communications with him. She felt that since he had been denied the adoption, he probably should not be part of my life.

That was when my life began to change. At age twelve I started to harden myself to everything and told myself I did not need a family, I needed to learn to survive without it. I had to figure out how to get what I needed without getting hurt again, because every time I opened up to someone, every time I trusted someone, something bad happened. I built a wall around myself a mile deep, which was partly a good thing I guess because it helped me survive some of those terrible foster homes over the years.

After I graduated from high school I got into a long-term relationship with someone and I allowed myself to believe in family for a while. We got married, but eventually we got divorced and through that I learned that getting married was probably the worst thing I could have done. I learned a lot of negative things because of the divorce, as it got very nasty, and I learned that family can hurt you in many ways. I still deal with a lot of trust issues because of everything.

It is interesting that my former music teacher who tried to adopt me when I was twelve offered to adopt me again when I was twenty, but I had become so closed off over the years I did not want to do it. I basically told him I never had a family and didn't need one, and I didn't want to strap him down like that. It wasn't until after I started working with a foster care organization, a national network of former and current foster kids that worked for the benefit of kids in foster care, that I started to change this view. They actually took a broken kid like me and turned me around. Before I started working with that organization, I looked at myself and saw an ugly person with a lot of anger and sadness, but working with them helped me see things differently. I was valuable, and I was worthy of love, worthy of a family.

I still stayed in touch with my former music teacher over the years as a mentor, and the relationship evolved. Around age twenty-five something seemed to change with me, the world became a little less gray and a little more black and white. I realized that I was not going to live forever and that I needed human connections to survive, so I finally opened myself up to adoption. My former sixth-grade music teacher became my adoptive dad when I was twenty-five. He had always been there for me, and he knew everything about me. When I was young and destructive, I tried to scare him away, so told him every dark secret whether appropriate or inappropriate to try to scare him away, and he just listened. He accepted me no matter what and never told me not to do something, and he always told me he saw something in me that other people did not. Through it all, he just stuck with it and told me he will always be there for me no matter what.

I am older now and through my work in Washington have the chance to really do some amazing things. I moved here to get away from the same community I lived in for thirteen years where everyone knew my story, and because I needed a fresh start. In Montana, I had done a lot of service through organizations to help foster kids, but I had never technically been employed in the child welfare area. A few years ago I was fortunate enough to combine my passion for changing the foster care system with my education and profession, and this led me to Washington. With this job, this is the first time I have technically been in a paid role working in foster care policy. I did advocacy and similar things as a volunteer, but this is the real thing, you know, getting paid to do it. Today, I look at where I came from and where I am now, and I think a lot of it was luck. I also think a lot of it had to do with the unconditional support I received from my mentor and now adoptive father over the years, and I feel so fortunate that I found a family and accepted it.

John
Montana

I am the adoptive father of Schylar. I first met Schylar when he was in the sixth grade and I was his music teacher. He moved to our area that year. I remember he was the tallest kid in the class and I noticed his potential early on. I had started something with the kids in elementary school to motivate them for the middle school talent show, giving them ideas based on their interests and talents, so they would be thinking early and preparing for the sixth-grade talent show. For example, a third grader would come up to me and tell me she was taking piano lessons, and I would say, "Oh, that is great because in sixth grade, I want to hear a great song from you in the talent show." By the time they got to the sixth grade, they wanted to win the talent show. Then, here came this tall transfer kid into the sixth grade. I asked him whether he had talents like dancing or singing, and he said no.

Being a foster kid had been really tough for him. The foster program should have given him the chance for outside things, like music and singing, but did not because he was moved from school to school and home to home. So, I told him I needed an assistant director for the talent show. He would need to make sure the kids, their costumes, music and everything else would be ready for the show. With Schylar as my assistant director, it turned out to be one of the best programs ever. He was absolutely wonderful, so he was very good in that assistant director role. He had a lot of skills in organization clear back to sixth grade. I was very proud of him.

There were some troubles with one of the foster homes Schylar was in at the time. Later, he told me upsetting things about that home. Once, they were to go to a resort area for a weekend. Before they left, another child in the home ran downstairs and made a mess in Schylar's bed, and then showed the foster parents as if Schylar had done it. They were furious and made Schylar stay home and miss the trip. He was ordered to wash all of the bed sheets in the house by the time they returned. This occurred many times, something would happen and he would have to stay home, clean the toilets or do something else.

Schylar had no one to go to at the time. Most foster kids don't in that type of situation. He would call me, and he tried hard not to be in tears, but I could tell he was crying. I often took him out for ice cream, just to get him out for a bit, and he told me about different things that were going on. I did not realize at the time that I was a mentor, but here was this kid who needed help and I would help him.

When Schylar was in the eighth grade, he was having troubles in a different foster home as well. Another child in the home had been getting into the family liquor cabinet and going to school drunk in the mornings. Schylar knew about it but felt he could not say anything to anyone. He was worried he would be blamed for it, because regardless of what happened he felt he was the one always blamed. That was the easiest way to find blame for something that was going on, so Schylar wouldn't say anything.

Schylar also told me that another kid in the home would get his buddies together and beat up on him. Schylar would roll up like a ball so they wouldn't kick him in the face. On one occasion, Schylar and he got into a tussle and pretty soon this kid was beating Schylar up inside the van. He grabbed Schylar and yanked him out onto the school lawn. This other kid was taking his revenge and hate out on Schylar, and it took all of the teachers that were around at that time to run over and grab this huge kid off of Schylar. That was the last straw and the foster care program finally decided they should take Schylar out of that home and move him to another one.

By the time Schylar was in senior high he had changed foster homes again. He loved music, so he came over to my house for piano, voice and acting lessons. He got to be quite good and was in some of the plays at a local theater besides being in things at school. During the lessons, I learned that this foster home was not so good either. He called the foster parent in this home a "Bible thumper," and I soon learned why. He came over one time with a huge black eye. He told me when he didn't do something they wanted him to do, they would grab the Bible and hit him with it.

It seems that for several families Schylar stayed with in foster care, and there were many, he went to a different church. Whenever he went to a new church, they told him the church he was last in was not the right one and he would need to be baptized again. Schylar has been baptized at least four or five times. As far as Schylar and religion go, he believes in God and the Trinity, but after everything he went through, he is not comfortable with all of it. I am Lutheran, and I would love to see him go to the Lutheran church.

During one year in high school the class was learning about the Salem witch trials and he brought a book home on Wickham. The foster family went berserk, yelling about his bringing that evil book into the house. They set fire to that book in the alley garbage can. It eventually got so bad at that home that Schylar packed up everything he owned in a duffel bag and ran out of the house. He called me later that day and said he was running away because he couldn't stand it anymore. He didn't want to be found, so he would be a street kid. I asked him if he had any money and he said no, so I gave him some when I met him in a parking lot. He wanted me to get out of there quickly so no one would connect us, so I drove on as if nothing happened.

He found some friends to live with and, of course, the police were looking for him. As he was coming out of a café downtown, the police found him. He lay down on the ground screaming, kicking and began yelling, "I'm crazy, I'm crazy." They took him to the psych ward, but he was only there for a short time. While in the psych ward, he started helping other people do various things like chores, and one of the workers noticed and asked him why he was there since he didn't seem mentally ill. He told her that if he was forced to go back to that foster home, he would show everyone what crazy is.

Foster care then sent him to a group home about three hours away from here. I tried to keep in contact with him to see how he was doing. He called me periodically and had started public school there. Schylar ended up taking tests at his new school, covering two quarters of his junior year and did so well they let him move into his senior year. He was also working two jobs and then he opted out of foster care before his time was up. It was then he found out that every foster kid has a lawyer assigned to them. Foster parents receive money for the program, but they often don't tell the kids that they have a lawyer too.

As a senior in high school, Schylar was chosen to play the lead in the musical, Camelot. I was so proud of him. Before graduation, the local newspaper came in and interviewed many of the high school seniors, including Schylar. The next day, when he was in class, a note arrived saying he needed to report to the principal's office. He had never in his life had to report to the principal's office and he started panicking. He was wondering if he was still going to graduate. Was something wrong? Had someone said something about him? He went to the principal's office and the principal stood up and shook his hand, and said, "Congratulations!" He asked if Schylar had seen the paper yet that day. He had not. There was a full page on Schylar and his story on the front page. After that, everyone in the school said hello to Schylar in the halls and really started noticing him. When he walked across the stage for graduation, everyone stood up and clapped. He told me he felt the power of love at that point.

He went on to college and worked his way through on scholarships. He found them from all over and said that you have to turn hunting scholarships into a job, a full-time job. He would send fifty or sixty applications out and maybe get one or two responses back, but it was enough to keep him in college. He got his degree in communications, and I went to his graduation, along with my sister and mom. We were all very proud of him.

I had told him during college that when he graduated, I would take him to England and show him Oxford where I went to school for a bit. We were both busy, so it wasn't until after he had been working on his master's for a while that we finally got a break to go. We went to England and a friend of mine there showed us around. Back home, when he graduated with honors in his master's degree, I was there too.

Sadly, soon after that my mother passed away. She lived to be one hundred and one years old, an active lady right up to the end. It was a hard time for me and I decided to spend the summer with my English friend in Switzerland, just to get away. When I came back I called Schylar and asked if he still wanted to be adopted. He said yes, because he had always wanted a family. We had checked into it many years earlier when he was twelve, and again later, but we got excuses that he was too old, or that I was single, nothing worked out for us before. This time we got a lawyer who could certainly do it. So, I adopted Schylar when he was twenty-five.

He became part of my family then, just before Christmas, December twenty-third. The judge said it was the best thing that had ever happened there. The courthouse was filled with friends and we had a wonderful celebration. I am sure my mom would have been very pleased. God does wonderful things. In my life, He has made some very right angles. He let me adopt Schylar, and I listen to Him because he has steered me in the right direction at important times.

If I were to emphasize anything for foster care, I would emphasize that kids need respect and love. Kids come into the foster care program and they do not know what is going on. It is a mystery to them as much as it is to the families themselves. The family is getting money because this child is coming into their home, and too often the child gets little benefit from that. I would say that in addition to respect and love, the foster parents should listen to the kids, hear their stories, and find out what their feelings are too. We should be aware of past hurt feelings, feelings that will be coming back up after being yanked away from their families and homes. You know, they long for a family, just like Schylar longed for adoption. I wish I could have adopted him a lot earlier, but we ran into some obstacles. I am so proud of him and so glad he is part of my family now.

Nathaniel

Georgia

At thirteen, I had been in so many different foster homes, and it was very clear to me by the last home that it just was not going to work for me. I did not feel like we foster kids were exposed enough to the better families. Some of the experiences I had in foster homes mirrored the experiences I had with my biological family. It is one thing to live in a biological family setup where you are being abused, abandoned and neglected at different levels, but then to be pulled out of there and put in other situations where the same abusive and neglectful experiences occurred was terrible! So foster care was a struggle for me. By the time I was in my last foster home where the parents were over seventy years old and I did not have a connection with them, I decided I wanted something more.

There were several people along the way who really helped me, who really made a difference and made my life go in a different direction. I was about to turn fourteen and I saw a commercial on TV about a boys' home in the south part of South Carolina. I recall it was a black and white TV, and I can remember it well. After I saw the commercial I decided to call Sylvia, the director of a children's shelter I had been in many times over the years and told her that if she could get me into that boys' home I promised I would not run away again. I had tried many times to run away from the foster homes I was in. It all started with Sylvia. She knew the foster homes I had been in were not the best situations, but that was all they had available. The one place I had always felt comfortable was at that children's shelter with Sylvia. Unfortunately, it was just a temporary emergency shelter so I could not stay there. Sylvia just never gave up on me, and she was able to get me into the boys' home I saw on TV.

When I got there I met Clara and her husband Leonard; they were my house parents. My other house parents in previous homes had been very conservative, so I could not just be myself. They were always trying to shape me into what they wanted me to be, but Clara was different. We called her Aunt Clara. She had been a beautician in her previous work and became very allergic to the chemicals so had to stop that work. She developed an interest in working with kids in foster care, so she and her husband became house parents at the boys' home.

I think Clara was the one that sort of cracked my shell in terms of me allowing myself to trust someone, allowing her to come into my space. As you probably know, many kids in foster care have experienced very intense trauma. Trust is a big issue after that, and then when you go from one foster home to another, over and over, and you interact with all of these different foster parents, social workers and other people you just put up walls. You just don't want to talk with anyone.

The first thing Clara did that I thought was interesting was when we went to a fast food restaurant for breakfast. She bought me a sausage biscuit and did not require payment. She did not say, hey, you owe me this, or any of that. That was new for me. When I got a job, I tried to slide money under her door at the home, so I could pay her back. She asked, what is this for? I said, well, you bought me a sausage biscuit. She would not accept it. There was just something about her and the consistency of her actions that helped me to trust her.

My tutor Jean was another person who helped me tremendously and has remained in my life even up to this point. She was a tutor for me in middle and high school, and she was just very real. She did not treat me differently because I was in foster care. She would ask me how I was feeling and if I was okay, but she did not try to be like a psychotherapist to me. She did not make me feel like I was odd, you know. So, those three people, Sylvia, Clara and Jean were three who made a huge difference in my life.

There was another person who was inspiring to me. When I was at the boys' home, around age fourteen, I met an older woman in the community and she was very encouraging. She told me that she had heard about me and that I was hard on myself at school. I said, yeah, I am not reading well, and I don't do math very well. I am just trying to figure out what I can do. She cut an inspirational message out of the newspaper for me and wrote me a little letter. Over time I lost the letter, but I still carry that little newspaper clipping around in my wallet to this day. It is really tattered since I have had it for over twenty years, but I keep it with me because it still inspires me. Sometimes I must read things like this to keep myself from being depressed.

Generally, I think state agencies have the best intentions to protect children, but in trying to do what is necessary for their safety, the kids never learn what it is like to be normal. They do not learn what it is like to have a family, how to take care of themselves, or how to prepare for when they leave the foster care system and must live on their own. The kids just don't have the support they need. I did not realize it at the time, but when I was in school I would adopt people psychologically and emotionally because I just did not have the family support I needed. When I found someone who was authentic, someone who did not seem to want to take something from me or use me, like a teacher or social worker, I would sort of unofficially adopt them emotionally. I clung to teachers and school counselors who really believed in what I was doing and didn't rush me.

I recall one school counselor, Amy, was very interested in me and she would ask me to think about what I wanted to do in life. I responded, "I live in foster care. What do you mean, what do I want to do? How do I know? Where am I going to live? What kind of resources am I going to have?" But there was something about how she said, *we will get to that when it's time*, that helped alleviate my stress and fear about what I would do when I needed to leave foster care. That was so helpful, because anxiety is already high for anyone getting ready to leave high school, but just imagine how it is for those who do not have any role models or support, no one to teach them how to be independent and answer some questions. So, I think being involved with some of those people, some of my teachers and counselors, gave me a sense of hope. It does not need to be about finding an exact answer or way to go, but just to have hope that something is possible, that something more is out there.

When I finally left the foster care system I became an investigator of my own life. I wanted to try to figure out family health issues. You know, doctors always ask about family medical history and I did not know mine. I wanted to find my birth certificate and social security card. I wanted school records, and I wanted to find some pictures of me as a child. I did not have any pictures and still do not. Not knowing or having these things can be hurtful, but I think the hardest piece is not having someone to call me on my birthday, not having a mother or father to call me.

I usually just spend my birthdays at home by myself. It is those things that are important, like birthdays and graduations and you want someone to celebrate your accomplishments. This helps you keep going. When you don't have the support, it is hard.

So for me, as I have gotten older I value everything, even the little things. I value cards I receive, and anything that symbolizes or represents some type of relationship, some type of connection with someone. I think for any of us who went through foster care, who went through such trauma, neglect and abandonment, we long for that connection with someone, someone who will just treat us as human beings. We want someone in our lives who will give us a hug or a pat on the back, just some type of affirmation that we are worthy, and we are loved.

I often try to reflect on where I came from. This is one way for me to center myself and appreciate things or practice gratitude. I don't want to forget where I came from, but I also don't want to get stuck in the past because it was so hard. You know, I still have physical scars from the trauma I experienced. They will not heal fully, they will always be there, but is it the physical scarring that I should pay most attention to? Or, is it the emotional and psychological scars I should pay the most attention to? I think the emotional and psychological issues are longer lasting. You can have surgery for the physical scars, grafts and other things to have them not show as much, but that internal stuff, that weighs on you.

I became a social worker and counselor, but I don't know that I actually chose social work and counseling because of what I experienced. I had my fair share of counselors and social workers, but not all of them were effective, so I think I chose this route because there was a lot of flexibility on where I could work and the things I could do. It also allowed me to advocate and to help people, to listen to them and help them make improvements and enhance their lives. I think I like that the most. You don't necessarily have to be an academic or be perfect in your analysis of someone, most people just want you to listen to them. They will tell you what you need to know, but most of them want you to listen and they want you to validate their experiences, good, bad and sad. I think people want the person who is listening to be more of a facilitator, someone who can help them think things through, to talk it out. I work with college students now as a counselor.

Sometimes I feel guilty for achieving success after foster care because I made it out and others did not. It is pretty common for someone who has gone through traumatic experiences to feel guilty if they make it out better than others. We know this from, for example, the holocaust where survivors felt guilty about their family members or friends not making it out. I think that happens with kids in foster care too. I think to myself, should I feel bad when I see that my buddies who were in the same group home were not as lucky as I was to make it out? Some of them are in prison and some of them are no longer alive, so that weighed heavily on me as I was trying to develop a sense of independence and identity.

Sometimes I go back to places where I was when I was younger, just to remind myself that all of that really did happen. Sometimes our experiences can just be so much that we wonder if all of it was real. I requested my records from the court and there was about one hundred and eighty pages worth of information on my case, on who would not pay child support and who did not want to take the blood test to prove fatherhood and all the rest. When you read that in black and white, you know it was not a dream. So, the question was, since this happened to me, what do I do with it? Therapy was important to me. I have been to quite a bit of therapy, but I don't look at therapy as being a place of detriment, I look at it as support. It gives you a space to be able to talk, to share, and to challenge yourself. It teaches you how to cope. If I am ever in the place where I think I have arrived, that will not be good. I am awake, I can see, and I want to keep growing.

I really don't need that much. I am not interested in being rich or anything, but I think if I could just buy a little house, that will be great or have a little apartment downtown. I don't need to keep up with the Joneses, but I would like a little place someday.

I want to be near the water and sit on my porch and say hello to the neighbors. That is the life I want. I don't need stress from worrying about stocks and bonds. Also, travel is crucial. I love to travel. I have been to England, France, Belgium and Germany. When you have been through some stuff, and we all have, you need to get out there and celebrate, to enjoy what you have.

Epilogue

I really enjoyed meeting each person I interviewed for this book, and am very thankful they agreed to meet with me and speak publicly. I decided to work on this project after mentoring an older boy in foster care for the last few years. Before I became a mentor I had no idea of the unending challenges, obstacles and heartbreak these kids face. As of the writing of this book, there are over 430,000 children in foster care in the United States. I hope people will think more about these kids and take steps to help them. There are many ways to help, whether it be to donate, volunteer, or become a foster or adoptive parent.

In loving memory of Debbie

Debbie was a wonderful wife, tremendously loving mother and a good friend to many. She knew too well the good and bad (and terrible) of the foster care system. In the words of her daughter, "The light you brought into the world will forever live on in the love that you gave to us." I believe Debbie has found true peace now and she is with God.